Puffin Books

OUT OF THE PIT
Fighting Fantasy Monsters

Steve Jackson and Ian Livingstone

Edited by Marc Gascoigne

1982 saw the publication of the first Fighting Fantasy Gamebook. *The Warlock of Firetop Mountain* by Steve Jackson and Ian Livingstone was an adventure of such intricacy and complexity that many readers have still to complete it successfully. It went straight into the bestseller lists. Since then, a whole series of Fighting Fantasy Gamebooks has been published and each one has become an instant bestseller.

What is the secret of their success? Some say it is the skilful construction of the adventures and the way the authors' devious minds create nasty traps for the unwary traveller to fall into. For some it is the freedom to roam a whole entirely believable fantasy world, and to venture across wild and dangerous lands in search of fame and treasure. But for most adventurers it is the monsters, the nightmare creatures which lurk in the deepest pools and in the darkest dungeons, that have made Fighting Fantasy into a truly world-wide phenomenon!

Out of the Pit is packed full of these loathsome creatures – some of them old adversaries, some we have yet to meet. Carefully illustrated, alphabetically arranged, with full statistics, notes on habitat and behaviour, and encounter tables, this book provides an indispensable guide for all Fighting Fantasy adventurers.

Steve Jackson and Ian Livingstone are the co-founders of the hugely successful Games Workshop chain and also creators of the whole Fighting Fantasy series. Marc Gascoigne is a seasoned adventurer and works on the production of many of the Games Workshop games.

FIGHTING FANTASY MONSTERS
OUT OF THE PIT

Steve Jackson and Ian Livingstone

Edited by Marc Gascoigne

PUFFIN BOOKS

For C. N.

Puffin Books, Penguin Books Ltd, Harmondsworth, Middlesex, England
Viking Penguin Inc., 40 West 23rd Street, New York, New York 10010, U.S.A.
Penguin Books Australia Ltd, Ringwood, Victoria, Australia
Penguin Books Canada Ltd, 2801 John Street, Markham, Ontario, Canada L3R 1B4
Penguin Books (N.Z.) Ltd, 182–190 Wairau Road, Auckland 10, New Zealand

First published 1985

Made and printed in Great Britain
Filmset in Palatino by Tradespools, Frome, Somerset

CONTENTS

INTRODUCTION

Fighting Fantasy fanatics are constantly writing to us with suggestions for new, blood-curdling monsters. Many ask us to tell them more about those which have already been featured in the gamebooks. Whereabouts in the world of Titan do they live? Who are their allies and enemies? Do they all eat human flesh? Which are the most fearsome?

We decided that there was only one way to answer all these questions in a logical and coherent way – extract all the monsters from the gamebooks and examine our creations much as Baron Frankenstein might. The resulting list was surprisingly long: we had invented well over 200 vile creatures with which to strike terror into the hearts of adventurers.

Having assembled our army of death, we thought that it deserved to be unleashed on the world, so we compiled a book of monsters which could be used as a warning to all adventurers who might otherwise think that only Orcs, Dragons, Ghouls and Zombies stalk the land. Within these pages ever-growing numbers of hideous mutants lie in wait for the foolish; Bloodbeasts, Death Wraiths, Shapechangers, Lizard Men and Ganjees are just a few.

We would like to thank Marc Gascoigne for his excellent editing work in the compilation of this book. His creative efforts have developed some of our original monsters and enabled them to fit properly into the world of Fighting Fantasy. At last they are ready to emerge in all their gruesome glory from *Out of the Pit*.

THE LAND OF DANGER

These are brutal, savage times. Much of the world of Titan is unsettled, explored only by brave warriors in search of adventure. Once there was a great civilization which covered the lands with roads and cities. The people of those past times were ruled over by mighty sorcerers, but the cataclysmic War of the Wizards put an end to order, and much of the world was overwhelmed by the armies of Chaos. Nowadays the remains of such people are found scattered everywhere: ruined towers and dungeons, villages and towns, even whole cities lie abandoned and overgrown, home only to ferocious monsters.

There are still sorcerers, but their arts have been twisted and debased through the centuries, and they have forgotten much of what their ancestors knew. Their ignorance makes their magic all the more dangerous, for they are unaware of the deadly nature of the grisly things they release into the world. As a consequence, most wizards and sorcerers are greatly feared.

In scattered corners across the world, isolated pockets of what passes for civilization have begun to re-emerge. Separated from one another by inhospitable wildernesses, they have become havens for all manner of barbaric and dangerous beings, both human and otherwise. New heroes have sprung up, ready to risk their lives in pursuit of fame and fortune. The most notorious of all lands is Allansia, a wild country of plains and hills, whose perils have been made infamous by the songs of minstrels.

Allansia is cut off, surrounded on all sides by inhospitable terrain. To the north are the frozen peaks of the Icefinger Mountains, to the south the burning expanses of the Desert of Skulls. The gale-swept Windward Plain leads out to the east towards the Flatlands, its seemingly endless wilds stalked by inhuman tribes and littered with prehistoric remains. And to the west there are the oceans, forever lashed with storms, and roamed by huge monsters which can swamp ships and drown sailors in an instant. Galleys ply up and down the coast from Port Blacksand, but only the desperate or the foolhardy dare venture out across the Western Ocean.

Of those who have attempted the crossing, few have survived the voyage and even fewer the passage back. Those who have returned have done so in despair, bringing with them the news that Chaos also reigns across the ocean in the land of Kakhabad. Travelling inland, adventurers have found themselves unable to explore the whole continent: the way north is blocked by the Zanzunu Peaks, south leads to the treacherous Jabaji River, and in the west the Cloudcap Mountains bar all further progress.

If you were ever to visit Allansia or Kakhabad, you would quickly understand why few people there reach their thirtieth year . . .

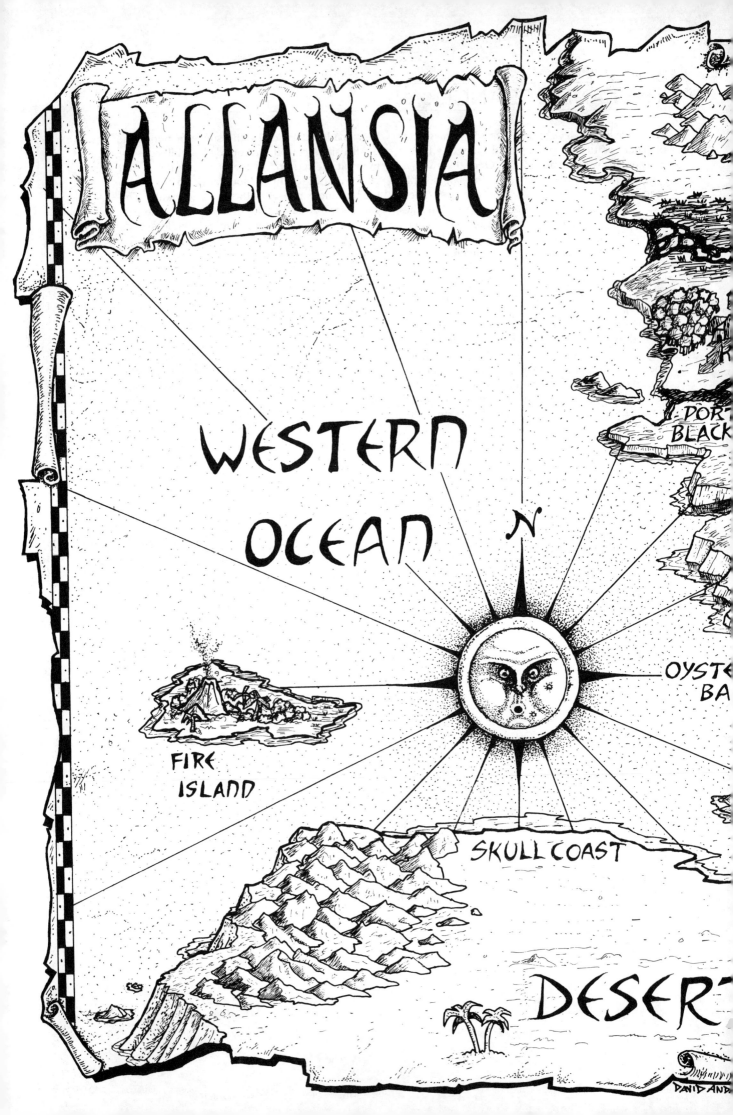

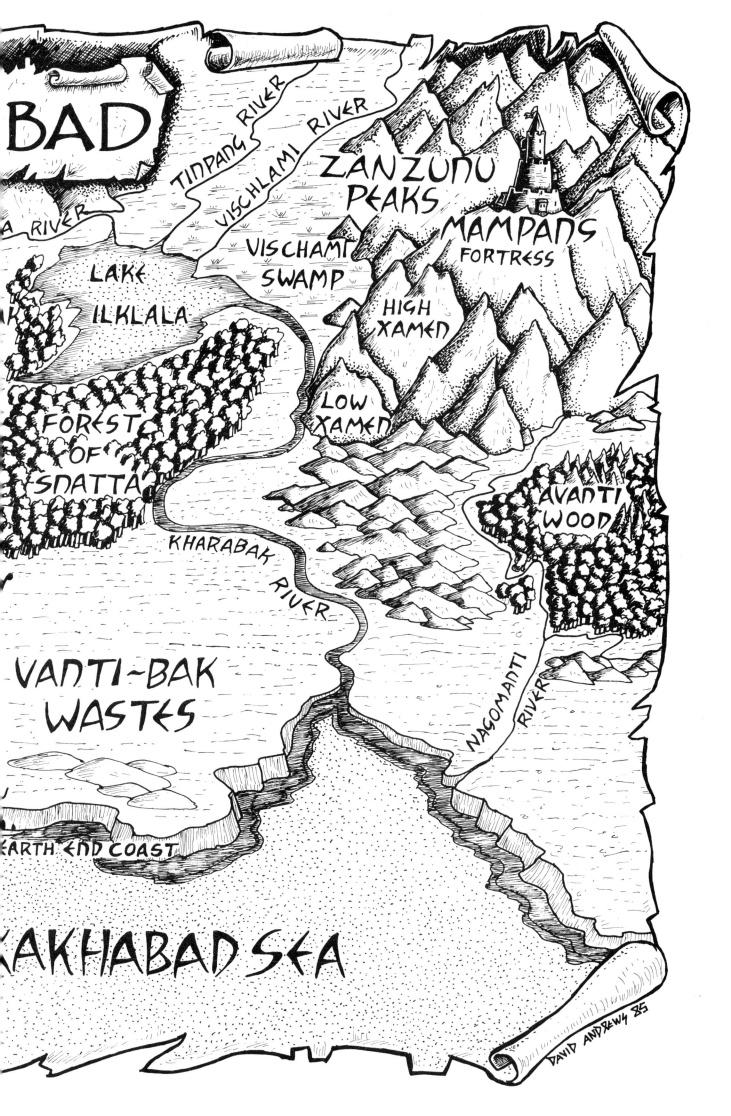

THE CREATURES OF ALLANSIA AND BEYOND

On the pages that follow you will find details of some of the fearsome monsters, humanoids and animals that can be encountered in the savage lands of Allansia and beyond. You can use them in designing your own adventures as a solo player, or players of *Fighting Fantasy – The Introductory Role-playing Game* may find themselves coming up against them in new adventures designed by their GamesMaster. Let us hope your swords remain sharp and your STAMINA is good . . .

In each of the entries that follow there are two sections – one lists the statistics for the creature for ease of reference, while the other consists of a longer description of the creature and its special features. The list for each creature provides the following details:

1. SKILL and STAMINA. These are average values, as not all creatures of the same species are exactly alike. In a large group of the creatures there will be some variation in these scores. For example, in a band of four Goblins, two may be typical creatures with SKILL 5, STAMINA 5; one might be the leader of the group, with SKILL 6, STAMINA 6; the last might be a little weaker, with only SKILL 4, STAMINA 3. Scores should only be varied by one or two points.

2. NUMBER OF ATTACKS. Solo players may ignore this score, as it is only used in a multi-player game. In most cases there are no details of the number of Attacks, which means that the creature has only a single Attack. Otherwise, the number given indicates the maximum number of opponents that a creature can fight in one Attack Round. If the creature has more Attacks than there are adventurers, it does not get any *extra* Attacks. Each Attack will be conducted from the single Attack Strength rolled for the creature, unless it says otherwise in the creature's description.

3. HABITAT. This indicates the general area a creature may be encountered in. Where more than one type of habitat is listed, the first is where the creature is most often found, the second where it is less frequently found, and so on. For example, Giant Eagles live mostly in mountainous areas, but they may also sometimes be encountered in hilly or wilderness areas.

The terms should be self-explanatory, but the following may help a GamesMaster when placing monsters in his adventures. *Towns* includes villages and other settlements. *Ruins* are found above ground, and can include towers, castles, houses and so on. *Dungeons*, on the other hand, are found below ground, and will not include natural caves. *Plains* are wide, generally grassy areas such as the Pagan Plain. *Wilderness* means large dead areas which are rocky and desolate, such as the Windward Plain or the fringes of the Desert of Skulls.

Demonic or *Magical Plane* refers to a supernatural home in another dimension; there are further explanations of these in the individual descriptions of the creatures.

4. NUMBER ENCOUNTERED. These numbers show how many creatures between one and three adventurers will encounter. If there are more players, their GamesMaster should feel free to double or treble the number they meet. Some beings are solitary creatures, however, and will only be encountered on their own: the description of the particular creature will have further information in these cases.

Rolling the numbers is simple: *1–6* means roll one die, and that many creatures are encountered; *2–12* means roll two dice, *3–18* means roll three dice, and so on. *1–3* means roll one die and halve the result, rounding any fractions *up*. *1–2* means roll one die: if the result is an odd number the score is 1, if it is even the score is 2. There are also a few other special numbers, which are explained in the descriptions of the monsters concerned.

5. TYPE. This gives a rough indication of the nature of the monster, and is also used to generate Treasure for it (see page 125).

6. REACTION. When adventurers first encounter a creature it will react to them in one of a number of ways. If it is *Friendly*, it greets them warmly and shows no hostility. It may share food or provide useful information for the adventurer(s). If it is *Neutral*, it is wary of them, but does not show open hostility; it will probably react if attacked, but may be fairly friendly if treated carefully. If it is *Unfriendly*, it shows obvious displeasure at encountering them, but does not leap into battle immediately; it may wait to sum up the situation before deciding one way or the other. If it is *Hostile*, this often means it is hungry! The creature will attack immediately. You will notice that for a few creatures two or more of these reactions are listed together. In these cases the creature may react either way, depending perhaps on what the adventurers are doing.

7. INTELLIGENCE. This final detail shows how clever a creature is. There are four scores for this: *High*, *Average*, *Low* and *None*. Humanoids will generally be rated as High (humans come somewhere in the middle of this category). Most monsters and some animals will be Average; the rest are Low. In general only plants have no intelligence at all. Intelligence should be borne in mind when considering the reaction of a particular creature. Clever beings will obviously use more cunning in their attack, and may even have spells or special weapons which they can use. Stupider creatures are more likely just to leap into battle regardless!

AAKOR

SKILL: 7
STAMINA: 8
HABITAT: Wilderness, Hills
NUMBER ENCOUNTERED: 2–7 (1 die plus 1)
TYPE: Animal
REACTION: Hostile
INTELLIGENCE: Average

AAKOR were perhaps once ordinary Wolves, before they gained their wings and their penchant for warm blood. It is more likely, though, that they are the remnants of some sorcerous experiment by a forgotten wizard centuries ago.

They are strange creatures, smaller than Wolves, but physically very similar, except for a large pair of feathery wings sprouting from their shoulders. They can fly well, steering themselves with their bushy tails as their keen eyes seek out suitable food below them. They hunt in packs, soaring high in the sky on outstretched wings and howling in the moonlight. They usually live on deer or boar, but they don't restrict their diet to four-legged creatures. They can prove dangerous foes, as they swoop down on travellers, claws outstretched to grab their next meal. They will take one particular target each, land on their prey and bite deeply. Once their prey has been finished off, they will pause to lap up the still-warm blood before tearing them apart and eating them.

GIANT AARDWOLF

SKILL: 7
STAMINA: 7
HABITAT: Plains, Wilderness
NUMBER ENCOUNTERED: 1–6
TYPE: Animal
REACTION: Neutral–Unfriendly
INTELLIGENCE: Low

GIANT AARDWOLVES are found only on the warm southern plains, where they roam in small groups. Related to hyenas, they are about the size of a large Wolf, but much leaner. Their short coats are yellow-grey, with irregular black stripes that help them hide in the long grasses. They normally eat insects, but they will defend themselves when threatened by large creatures. If more than three are encountered, the others will be cubs (SKILL 4, STAMINA 3). The adults will be more vigilant and protective, and will attack to guard their young.

GREAT APE

SKILL: 8   2 Attacks
STAMINA: 11
HABITAT: Forests, Jungles, Hills, Caves, Wilderness
NUMBER ENCOUNTERED: 1–2
TYPE: Animal
REACTION: Unfriendly–Hostile
INTELLIGENCE: Low

GREAT APES look very much like huge hairy Gorillas, about two and a half metres tall and almost as broad. They are not confined to tropical regions, and may be encountered in all kinds of wild terrain. They are carnivorous beasts, delighting particularly in eating the tender flesh of humans. They attack with their huge fists, which are so strong that they can punch through armour! Great Apes typically make their lairs in old caves, or at the top of large trees, from where they swing out through the branches each day in search of food.

Although most Great Apes are unintelligent, aggressive brutes, there are a few remarkable species which have developed in isolation in a remote corner of Kakhabad. For more details of the Apes of Mauristatia, see the appropriate sections on Champaque, Howl Cat, Mungie and Wraith Ape.

APE MAN

SKILL: 8
STAMINA: 7
HABITAT: Forests, Jungles
NUMBER ENCOUNTERED: 1–2
TYPE: Humanoid
REACTION: Hostile
INTELLIGENCE: Average

Life in the thick forests of Allansia and beyond is not restricted to ground level. High in the trees live many agile creatures which moved upward originally to escape predators. In time, however, the predators followed them, and the tree-tops are as dangerous as the ground. From huts built on platforms perched in the crooks of large branches, brutish APE MEN, the largest predators in the trees, swing far and wide on vines rigged up like ropes, on the trail of food.

They are huge hair-covered humanoids, related to Neanderthals and Cavemen and usually dressed in little more than an animal-hide loincloth; they carry a large bone club. They are omnivorous, eating the meat of small forest creatures as well as fruit and berries, depending on what they can find as they travel about their leafy domain. Ape Men are very agile and can swing on the thinnest of branches or hang by one hand. Anyone who tries to fight them while perched up a tree, however, must reduce his Attack Strength by 2 points to account for the precarious surroundings. In an Ape Man's lair, typically a tree-house woven from branches and carpeted with grass, there will be many bones and rotting fruit. There may also be a few cheap, brightly sparkling trinkets, for like most primitives Ape Men are attracted to objects that twinkle in the light.

BADDU-BEETLE

SKILL: 7   2 Attacks
STAMINA: 9
HABITAT: Wilderness, Plains
NUMBER ENCOUNTERED: 1
TYPE: Insect
REACTION: Unfriendly
INTELLIGENCE: Low

Taking their name from the Baddu-Bak Plains of Kakhabad where they were first encountered,

BADDU-BEETLES are ferocious predatory insects which can grow up to four metres long. It is the way they obtain their food that can be most alarming, however. These solitary hunters bury themselves in the earth and drag loose soil over themselves until no trace remains on the surface to betray their presence. When they hear the vibrations caused by another creature passing by, they burst out and grab at their prey with their huge serrated claws.

Once they have emerged from their burrow, they may be fought normally. However, whenever the creature is hit, it will angrily spit a virulent acid at its opponent. On a roll of 1–4 on one die, it will hit and burn away 2 STAMINA points. Once the Beetle has killed its prey, it will drag the corpse back into its burrow to be slowly digested.

BANSHEE

SKILL: 12
STAMINA: 12
HABITAT: Caves, Ruins
NUMBER ENCOUNTERED: 1
TYPE: Undead
REACTION: Hostile
INTELLIGENCE: Low

BANSHEES are hideous undead creatures often heard, but rarely met, in the desolate, forsaken wastelands in which they dwell. They are chiefly known for the soul-shredding wail that they constantly howl, both day and night, as they wander the wastes. The ghastly spectres are thought to be human spirits, trapped on this plane and unable to rest, as punishment for some horrific crime committed when they were alive.

In its new form, a Banshee appears as a shrivelled, knotted old man or woman, with long, unkempt hair, one large nostril and a single tooth. Its eyes are ringed red; all the creature's sorrow and anger is reflected in them, if anyone dares to look. In an attack, it will use its scaly, claw-tipped hands. Its screaming will prove very disturbing to its opponents, who must roll their SKILL or below on two dice at the beginning of each Attack Round, or be transfixed with fear until the next round. If opponents become petrified with fear in this way, they will be very easy targets for the Banshee's claw, which will automatically cause 2 points of STAMINA damage for each strike.

BASILISK

SKILL: 5
STAMINA: 8
HABITAT: Deserts, Plains, Ruins
NUMBER ENCOUNTERED: 1
TYPE: Monster
REACTION: Unfriendly
INTELLIGENCE: Low

From a distance it could be a large lizard, two metres from snout to tail, and coloured a mottled sandy-brown. Those innocent or foolish adventurers who want to get closer will notice that the creature's head is rather bird-like and is tilted from side to side as it tentatively sniffs the air. For one brief moment, they may take in the fact that its eyes are large and yellow, almost like a frog's, before the gaze of the BASILISK turns them to stone.

These legendary beasts kill by catching the gaze of their victim and petrifying them. An opponent needs to *Test for Luck* successfully in order to cover his eyes in time and avert his gaze. Attacking the creature by slashing a weapon at it without looking is just as perilous, for its poisonous breath will kill instantly! However, a Basilisk's gaze is as harmful to itself as it is to other living things. Should it catch sight of its eyes in a mirror or some other reflective device, it will turn itself to stone, hardening from living flesh to dead rock in an instant.

BAT

	Common Bat	Vampire Bat	Giant Bat
SKILL:	4	5	5
STAMINA:	4	4	8

HABITAT: *Caves, Plains, Forests, Ruins, Jungles*
NUMBER ENCOUNTERED:
   Common Bat – flock of 25–30 (24 plus 1 die)
   Vampire Bat – 1–3
   Giant Bat – 1
TYPE: *Animal*
REACTION: *Unfriendly*
INTELLIGENCE: *Low*

BATS, whatever their size or feeding habits, are found in most places across central and southern Allansia and Kakhabad. Typically coloured somewhere between light brown and dark grey, they look like nothing so much as flying mice, with a pair of leathery wings stretched out between their elongated front legs. Their ears are large in comparison to the rest of their heads, and help them fly in darkness by picking up echoes off solid objects around them.

COMMON BATS usually avoid creatures larger than themselves. They feed on mice, voles, insects and sometimes berries and fruit. They can be a hazard to an adventurer who suddenly disturbs a large number of them and finds himself being battered on all sides by a whole frightened flock! The whole flock can be treated as a single opponent: the Bats buffet with their wings, get tangled in hair or clothes, and so on. When their S T A M I N A score reaches zero, this indicates that the Bats have flown away and are no longer a threat, rather than that the adventurer has killed every single one of them!

VAMPIRE BATS are far more dangerous, for they are predatory creatures that live by sucking the blood of living things. They look much like normal Bats, though they are larger. They have greatly enlarged front teeth, which they will use to pierce the flesh of their victims. If there is more than one Vampire Bat involved in an attack, the other(s) will land on their opponent and automatically begin sucking 1 S T A M I N A point each per round, until he is killed.

GIANT BATS are only found in the warmer climate of the southern jungles, where they feed on monkeys, small deer and other similar creatures. Their wings span about two metres when fully extended, as the Bats soar high in the night sky. They are not afraid to attack humans, though fire will keep them at bay. Once they have killed their prey, they will carry it in their strong claws back to their caves to be eaten.

BEAR

	Adult	Cub	
SKILL:	9	5	2 Attacks
STAMINA:	8	6	

HABITAT: *Forests, Hills, Wilderness, Ice*
NUMBER ENCOUNTERED: 1–3
TYPE: *Animal*
REACTION: *Neutral–Unfriendly*
INTELLIGENCE: *Low*

Shy and secretive, BHORKET have only rarely been encountered by adventurers in the eastern forests where they dwell. These creatures are short (one and a half metres tall, at the most) and squat, but have long, powerful arms and legs. Bhorket look like apes, and are covered with shaggy pelts of brown-green hair, but are more closely related to Bears.

Bhorket are vegetarian herbivores, living on roots, berries and flowers, and they are peaceful, nervous creatures as a result. Because of this, and the fact that their flesh is apparently quite succulent and tender, they have long suffered the ravages of predators like lions and jackals. As a result, Bhorket have developed an incredible dexterity which allows them to leap up to ten metres with a single bound, and swing from tree to tree at incredible speed! Such tactics help them escape most threats.

Bhorket only mate once every four years or so, and thus are extremely protective of the single cub that results. At such times, a Bhorket couple will take turns at looking after the young, one staying behind while the other patrols the vicinity, wildly attacking any predators it encounters, to ensure the safety of the helpless cub. A young Bhorket is usually just like its parents; it will grow to maturity in about three years (adding 1 SKILL and 2 STAMINA each year until adulthood).

BEARS may be encountered by adventurers in many wild areas across the northern lands. Even in the ice-bound coastal regions north of the Icefinger Mountains, snow-white Polar Bears dwell. Most bears are omnivores – eating meat, fish, berries, plants and fruit, depending upon what they can find. If a Bear feels threatened, it will put on a very aggressive show of strength. Rising up on its hind legs, it will advance, growling warily, before attacking with teeth and claws. If more than one Bear is encountered, the others will be cubs, miniature replicas of their parent. The parent will make distinctly threatening noises towards anyone encountered, and may well attack immediately. Bears are very protective of their cubs, and will not wait to see whether they really are in danger before they attack. Good-quality bearskins will fetch a high price in most towns and larger villages, for they are used to make all sorts of fine clothes.

BHORKET

	Adult	Young	
SKILL:	8	5	Adults have 2 Attacks
STAMINA:	11	5	

HABITAT: Forests, Jungles
NUMBER ENCOUNTERED: 1–3
TYPE: Animal
REACTION: Neutral
INTELLIGENCE: Low

BIRD MAN

SKILL: 10
STAMINA: 8
HABITAT: Mountains, Hills
NUMBER ENCOUNTERED: 1–6
TYPE: Bird/humanoid
REACTION: Neutral–Unfriendly
INTELLIGENCE: Average–Low

Tribes of BIRD MEN are found in mountainous areas across the whole of Allansia and Kakhabad, perched in villages and caves in the highest peaks.

They are short and sinewy, with especially powerful chest muscles, which support a wide pair of feathered wings. Their mouths are sharp, hooked beaks, and both arms and legs end in cutting talons. They are covered in short, almost feathery hair, which varies in colour from green through brown to grey and black, according to their tribe. Bird Men talk in strange chirruping voices that can change into disconcerting piercing shrieks as they wheel down out of the sky to attack their foes.

The tribes of the Moonstone Hills in northern Allansia are quite primitive for their race. Attracted by metal objects, which they consider great status symbols, they will attack lone adventurers in great numbers. They are rather cowardly creatures, though, and a display of strength by their victim can often drive them off in search of easier prey!

The Bird Men of northern Kakhabad's Zanzunu Peaks are more civilized, and dwell in large labyrinthine towns carved into the sides of the impassable peaks. The rise in power of the Archmage in Mampang split the tribes, and civil war rages between them even now. Some sided with the sorcerer and became his troops, even stealing the legendary Crown of Kings from Analand for their evil new master. Others, however, declined to serve the magician, and now hide in well-defended settlements, mounting raids on the other tribes in planned guerilla actions. They can use crude spears and swords, and even fly in tight aerial formation.

They have been known to help adventurers by providing information or a lift over the inhospitable terrain, in return for news from the outlands or aid in the war against their enemies. If crossed by an ally of the evil Bird Men, however, their response will be swift and merciless. Their favourite punishment is to grab their prey by the limbs, climb high into the sky and then allow it to drop to its death on the rocks below.

BLACK LION

SKILL: 11
STAMINA: 11
HABITAT: Jungles, Plains
NUMBER ENCOUNTERED: 1
TYPE: Animal
REACTION: Unfriendly
INTELLIGENCE: Low

It is not known whether BLACK LIONS are the result of a wizard's experiment or natural cross-breeding in the wild. What is certain, however, is that they are a cross between a black panther and a lion, a mix that makes them the most savage of all the hunting cats. These deadly predators are found where the grasses of hot plains meet the thick vegetation of jungles. They usually sleep all day, languishing in the crook of a branch high above the ground. Come twilight, they will descend from their lofty perch to hunt wild boar, deer and other nocturnal creatures. They can run, leap and climb well, and are consequently very dangerous to all creatures. Once a Black Lion is on the trail of its prey, there is little the hapless quarry can do to escape the beast's claws and teeth.

Some have tried to tame Black Lions, but with little success, for the creatures are as wild as enraged tigers. Occasionally, however, men have been able to separate some cubs from their mother, steal them and domesticate them for use as guards and pets. But Black Lions never remain loyal to any master for very long, and sooner or later turn on him and extract their revenge for their imprisonment.

BLOODBEAST

SKILL: 12
STAMINA: 10
HABITAT: Dungeons
NUMBER ENCOUNTERED: 1
TYPE: Monster
REACTION: Hostile
INTELLIGENCE: Low

There are a number of beasts that recur again and again in the bestiaries of sages and the cautionary tales of nursemaids; their powers become more and more exaggerated through the years. Some creatures, however, turn out to be just as black as they have been painted: one such is the BLOODBEAST.

This monstrosity is large, at least four metres long, and so bloated it can never leave the pool of foul slime that has supported its bulk since it was spawned. Its hide is tough and leathery, protected by thin spines and coloured a disgusting grey-green. Its head appears to consist of a myriad eyes above a vacant, toothy maw. The Bloodbeast's one major weakness has always been its two real eyes, so it has evolved hundreds of fake 'eyes' that rise in blisters before bursting open on its head. Anyone taking on the creature will need a lucky strike (*Test for Luck*) to hit its real eyes and pierce its brain. Attempting such a blow, however, means avoiding the thing's long, slimy, pink tongue. Unless its opponent can slash off the tongue with a dagger (by rolling his SKILL or less on two dice), he will be dragged into the pool, where the powerfully acidic slime will quickly decompose his body, until it is ready to be eaten!

WILD BOAR

SKILL: 6
STAMINA: 5
HABITAT: Forests, Plains, Hills
NUMBER ENCOUNTERED: 1–3
TYPE: Animal
REACTION: Unfriendly
INTELLIGENCE: Low

WILD BOAR are hunted for their choice meat and pelts in many areas across northern Allansia. They look like huge pigs, covered in tangled clumps of short brown hair. They are brutish, aggressive beasts, and will stand and fight with their tusks, if threatened, with an almost berserk fury. Occasionally, those encountered will be a single male and a number of smaller sows. In this case, the male will stand its ground, holding off danger while the others escape into the undergrowth. The pelt and meat of a fair-sized Boar can fetch a few Gold Pieces in the market-place of any village or town.

BOULDER BEAST

SKILL: 8
STAMINA: 11
HABITAT: Hills, Caves, Forests, Ruins
NUMBER ENCOUNTERED: 1
TYPE: Magical Creature
REACTION: Unfriendly–Hostile
INTELLIGENCE: Low

Men have always dabbled in things they don't fully understand. BOULDER BEASTS are thought to be the result of the ignorant meddling of a foolish elementalist. In trying to summon a major Earth Elemental from another plane to become his slave, he unwittingly also released a group of evil Earth Spirits, which were trapped here, unable to return.

The spirits inhabit large boulders, which they slowly propel around their rocky domains on short, stubby legs, their wide toes well suited to the rough ground. They feed, rather cannibalistically, on clumps of stone, which they tear away from larger outcrops with their huge stone fists. They will also use their hands in attacking any creature that disturbs them. Their rocky bodies will prove rather tough for swords, which will only deliver a single point of damage in a successful hit. A crushing weapon such as a mace or war-hammer will prove more deadly to a Boulder Beast, and will smash 3 points off the thing with every blow that connects.

When a Boulder Beast dies, its spirit will finally be released to return to its home plane, free at last.

BRAIN SLAYER

SKILL: 10   2 Attacks
STAMINA: 10
HABITAT: Dungeons
NUMBER ENCOUNTERED: 1
TYPE: Humanoid
REACTION: Hostile
INTELLIGENCE: High

Many are the references in the legends of the subterranean races to horrifically evil, horrendously foul-looking creatures called BRAIN SLAYERS. They dwell in isolated colonies deep in the earth, far below even the furthest explorations of the inquisitive Dwarfs, and rarely venture towards the surface. They detest light, warmth and indeed life itself; never was there a race more suited to darkness.

Even the most insane Demon would have trouble imagining a Brain Slayer. It is as though an octopus had somehow sprouted from the shoulders of a large, strong human body. Their skin is slick with slime and mucus, and is coloured a stomach-churning purple-green. As they move, their tentacles whip around in a frenzy, as if they were trying somehow to sniff out living creatures to feed upon. They dress in long flowing robes patterned with bizarre designs. To look into the eyes of a Brain Slayer, it is said, is to gaze into pure, unsullied hatred.

Their eyes carry their most potent weapon – a powerful hypnotic gaze that can transfix a man and swiftly draw him into the range of their tentacles. Anyone encountering a Brain Slayer must successfully *Test for Luck* twice, or be hypnotized. The creature will enfold the victim in its rank, slimy tentacles and feed greedily upon his mental energy – he will lose 1 SKILL point, and one die of STAMINA damage from such a hit. After the first, incredibly agonizing strike, the hypnosis will be broken, though, and the victim can attack as normal against the flailing tentacles. If it finds itself losing, a Brain Slayer will attempt to flee, for ultimately they are cowardly creatures.

BRISTLE BEAST

SKILL: 5
STAMINA: 7
HABITAT: Plains, anywhere men are
NUMBER ENCOUNTERED:
    Wild – 1–6
    Tame – 1
TYPE: Animal
REACTION: Friendly–Unfriendly
INTELLIGENCE: Low

BRISTLE BEASTS are most commonly encountered as pets, belonging to well-travelled or rich city-dwellers in Blacksand or Kharé. They are lizard-like creatures, growing to the size of a large dog, and covered in thousands of short, sharp spines. They originally come from the warm plains of the southern lands, where they live in burrows dug in the sandy earth. They eat small mammals and insects, which they will often play with before killing, just like a cat. They can be domesticated, if training starts early enough, and will prove loyal and obedient, provided they are fed and cared for. They will never permit themselves to be leashed, though they can be trained to walk close at heel when accompanying their owner in the street. They are especially useful as guard-animals, for they will ferociously attack any intruder – their spines erect, hissing through their teeth, pacing warily before an opponent before striking with their claws. If necessary, they will fight to the death for their master, though their owner will usually try to stop the fight before that happens, for they are rare and expensive beasts.

CAARTH

	Adult Male	Adult Female	Young
SKILL:	10	8	4
STAMINA:	11	9	5

HABITAT: *Wilderness, Deserts*
NUMBER ENCOUNTERED: *2–7 (1 die plus 1)*
TYPE: *Humanoid*
REACTION: *Hostile*
INTELLIGENCE: *High*

Beyond the southern limits of human civilization lie endless desert wastes. Here and there are scattered tribes of squat Ape Men and brutish Neanderthals, but ruling over this inhospitable domain are the CAARTH, the Serpent Warriors. Legend says they are descended from the same lineage as men and Orcs; but where man came from apes and Orcs were crossed with swine, the Caarth are the result of a sorcerous experiment with snakes!

Standing over two metres tall, these evil humanoids have blunt reptilian heads, crowned with a bony ruff at the back of the neck, which leads

down to a ridged, spiny back. Cold, cruel eyes bulge from the top of their snouts, and their mouths are full of needle-like fangs. Their bodies and limbs are smooth and hairless, but their hands and feet end in bestial talons. When patrolling their extensive lands, they ride large lizards, which are trained in fighting.

Caarth are highly intelligent, and their knowledge is said to be as wide as man's. They are much stronger than men, however, and are fearless warriors, fighting with teeth and talons as well as sword, javelin and bow. The Caarth armies are strong and disciplined, and have spread cruel dominion over much of the southern land, taking slaves and high taxes of all they rule. They are kept from spreading further north only by the more temperate climate (like lizards, they are cold-blooded); on the margins of civilization, however, their raiding parties burn villages and attack trading caravans, leaving survivors staked out in the sand for the scorpions and vultures to feast on.

In their labyrinthine stone cities, hidden deep in the wastelands, they are ruled over by mighty demonic sorcerers and high priests; all worship the Snake Demon Sith. Tales of their jewelled temples and mystic libraries have long driven adventurers to attempt to reach these cities. A few survivors of such expeditions have been found wandering the desert, parched and starving. Turned insane by the sun, they babble of gleaming daggers, claws dripping poison, and snakes, snakes everywhere . . .

CALACORM

SKILL: 9   2 Attacks
STAMINA: 8
HABITAT: *Caves, Wilderness, Dungeons, Ruins, Towns*
NUMBER ENCOUNTERED: *1–3*
TYPE: *Humanoid*
REACTION: *Unfriendly*
INTELLIGENCE: *Average*

CAT PEOPLE

SKILL: 8
STAMINA: 6
HABITAT: Forests, Hills, Plains
NUMBER ENCOUNTERED: 1–3
TYPE: Animal/humanoid
REACTION: Neutral–Unfriendly
INTELLIGENCE: Low

The CAT PEOPLE of central Allansia are a strange race of primitive humanoids related to felines. Their heads are cat-shaped, with human features offset by slanting green eyes, long teeth and whiskers. They have paws instead of hands and feet, which are equipped with sharp, retractable claws. They are covered in a smooth pelt of short black fur. They are very dextrous, and may sometimes be seen springing between the branches of trees at twilight, on the trail of their prey. They live on the small creatures they can catch, though they are not afraid of taking on larger beings, even humans.

Possibly related to Lizard Men, with which they share many physical similarities, CALACORMS are strange reptilian humanoids often found in the service of an evil leader. They are about two metres tall, covered completely in grey scales, and have very long tails, which drag along behind them. Bizarrely, the creatures also have two heads, which chatter to each other the whole time. They are strong but simple creatures, who are content and reliable as long as their needs are catered for. If they have a plentiful supply of their favourite food (dead snakes!), a comfortable room, and the occasional prisoner to torture when they want entertainment, they will follow their master to Hell if need be.

They can speak the language of men, though with both heads talking at once it is often difficult to understand what they say. If they are in the employ of someone, they will be carrying a sword or spear, with which they will fight skilfully. Their strength, and the coordination the two heads give them, make them redoubtable fighters. However, they are terrified of rodents – especially mice! When faced with one, a Calacorm will shriek with terror and hide in a corner until the little beast has gone. Why they do this is not clear, though an old legend talks of how a Lizard God, called Suthis Cha, choked to death while trying to devour the Mouse God Karreep. It is possible that the suspicious Calacorms fear that mice come seeking revenge for such a blasphemy against their Deity!

The origins of the Cat People are lost in the far distant past. Their own legends, told to curious scholars in their strange growling and mewing language, speak of a curse laid upon a race of cats by a malevolent sorcerer, a curse that has forced them to inhabit human bodies ever since. It is thought that their race was more populous in earlier times; nowadays only a handful of tribes remain, split into hundreds of small family groups across the land. Their numbers are threatened even more in recent times, for they are hunted for their pelts by unscrupulous poachers.

CAVEMAN

SKILL: 7
STAMINA: 7
HABITAT: Caves, Hills, Mountains, Wilderness
NUMBER ENCOUNTERED: 1–3
TYPE: Humanoid
REACTION: Hostile
INTELLIGENCE: Low

Related to Neanderthals, CAVEMEN are primitive semi-humans who live in rocky regions. Their caves are often joined together by passages to create whole villages cut into the rocky hillsides. They dress in the furs of animals, typically bearskins. Cavemen will usually be carrying stone clubs or flint-headed spears (these can be thrown, hitting on a roll of 1–3 on one die for 3 STAMINA points of damage).

Cavemen are very unintelligent, and communicate only in animal-like grunts. They will attack all other large beings, either for food or because they seem like a threat to them. Cavemen are surly, aggressive beings, and they tend to fight among themselves. There is almost always a war going on between two or more tribes, usually over some very trivial matter.

The caves of these beings are nauseously filthy, scattered with rotting food, old furs and discarded straw bedding. They will usually contain nothing of any worth to an adventurer.

Part man and part horse, CENTAURS look more like creatures out of a legend than real beings. They stand on four legs, for they have the bodies and hindquarters of horses. Above the waist, though, they appear to be normal humans. They are as intelligent as their two-legged relations, and may sometimes converse with them. They will usually be carrying bows, spears and shields. In times of war they may even wear full armour, including protection for their lower bodies. Centaurs dwell on the wide open plains found in many parts of the world, and roam in small hunting parties in search of food. They will eat both grass and meat, though they prefer the latter.

Centaurs have a completely different culture to humans, and many tribes relish attacking and eating humans with scant regard for their racial similarities. The beings believe themselves to be horses cursed for some misdeed by their great Stallion God Hunnynhaa, and forced to suffer the indignity of a sluggish human body. They delight in the telling and singing of tales that speak of their curse and their desire to be free of it. Young Centaurs are much like their parents, though smaller and very mischievous.

CENTAUR

	Adult	Young	
SKILL:	10	6	*Adults have 2 Attacks*
STAMINA:	10	5	

HABITAT: Plains, Wilderness, Forests
NUMBER ENCOUNTERED: 1–6
TYPE: Animal/humanoid
REACTION: Neutral–Unfriendly
INTELLIGENCE: High

GIANT CENTIPEDE

SKILL: 9
STAMINA: 7
HABITAT: Caves, Ruins, Dungeons, Jungles
NUMBER ENCOUNTERED: 1–2
TYPE: Insect
REACTION: Unfriendly
INTELLIGENCE: Low–None

GIANT CENTIPEDES can be found in many dank, desolate places. Up to four metres long, these monsters are covered in tough, bony plates of black, chitinous armour. They scuttle around at high speed on many tiny legs, which enable them to cope with all kinds of rough terrain. They are scavengers, feeding on dead meat and rotting vegetation, but will also chase and catch live food. The first indication of the presence of a Giant Centipede is a strange clicking noise, which is caused by the scales of its armour rubbing together as it rushes along. In an attack, if room permits, it will dart forward, raise itself on its hind legs and bite with its large, strong mandibles. Some jungle-dwelling species have poisonous bites, which will deliver an extra 2 points of damage to a successful bite. Such creatures are rare, thankfully, and dwell only in the far eastern lands, so that they are encountered only infrequently by man.

long, powerful limbs. The Champaque is a voracious carnivore which spends much of its time well hidden in the upper branches of its favourite tree, watching for prospective prey. It is a solitary creature and has the uncanny ability to mimic the voices of any animal it studies. Having such a close resemblance to humans, it can not only imitate a human voice, but can also mimic human mannerisms. For those who have never come across a Champaque before, it at first appears to be a curious hybrid of man and ape.

Its behaviour will be friendly, as it attempts to catch its victim off guard by continuing a conversation (but never giving much information away), until it seizes its chance to attack.

The purpose of its attack is always for food and it will drag its victim away as quickly as possible into the undergrowth where it will feast on the warm brain. After having eaten, the beast becomes even more dangerous. For the Champaque has the ability to digest parts of its victim's brain intact, thus absorbing some of the intelligence of its hapless prey. For each gruesome meal that a Champaque has eaten within the previous twenty-four hours, its SKILL increases by 1 point up to a maximum of 5, when it will be full. Thus a fully fed Champaque will be SKILL 12, STAMINA 10. The only advice that can be offered to adventurers who come across a Champaque is simple: it must be killed immediately!

CHAMPAQUE

SKILL: 7
STAMINA: 10
HABITAT: Hills, Mountains, Forests
NUMBER ENCOUNTERED: 1
TYPE: Animal
REACTION: Friendly (but see below)
INTELLIGENCE: Average

Easily recognizable by its long green fur, which serves to camouflage it well in the higher branches of Pango Trees, the CHAMPAQUE is a beast to be avoided at all costs. It is a moderately intelligent creature, with a face like an ageing sorcerer and

CHANGELING

SKILL: see below
STAMINA: see below
HABITAT: Dungeons, Ruins, Caves
NUMBER ENCOUNTERED: 1
TYPE: Magical creature
REACTION: Hostile
INTELLIGENCE: High

Malevolent Chaotic spirits can be found lurking in many dangerous parts of the underworld, waiting to trap any prey that might stumble into their domain. One of the most bizarre of all these beings is the CHANGELING, which can turn its form into that of another, more powerful being at will.

Its natural form is that of a tiny human baby, ideal for enticing its prey nearer, until it can strike. When first encountered, it will be lying in a cradle, crying its eyes out. If comforted the infant will appear to calm down and begin cooing to itself. As soon as it can, though, the creature will change its shape and attack. Its new form can be determined by rolling two dice on the following table:

Dice Roll	Form	SKILL	STAMINA	Attacks
2	Hill Giant	9	11	2
3	Werewolf	8	9	2
4	Cyclops	10	10	1
5	Nandibear	9	11	2
6	Doragar	9	10	1
7	Goblin	5	5	1
8	Ghoul	8	7	2
9	Minotaur	9	9	2
10	Cave Troll	9	10	2
11	Brain Slayer	10	10	2
12	Fire Demon	10	10	3

The beast will be exactly like its real counterpart, but it will not have any of its special features (a Ghoul's touch will not be poisonous, a Fire Demon can be hit by normal weapons, and so on). When the creature's STAMINA has been reduced to 4 points, the Changeling will take on another form, rolled again on the table. And when this second creature has been reduced to 4 STAMINA points, it will change again into its final form, indicated by a further roll on the table. This last form can be killed, the Changeling reverting to its normal form when it dies – a tiny, innocent baby.

CHESTRAP BEAST

SKILL: 5
STAMINA: 6
HABITAT: Dungeons
NUMBER ENCOUNTERED: 1
TYPE: Humanoid
REACTION: Unfriendly–Hostile
INTELLIGENCE: Average

Many an unwary adventurer has met a grisly end while opening a treasure chest. Poison needles, gas jets and venomous serpents are just a few of the perils one may encounter; possibly the most alarming, though, is the CHESTRAP BEAST.

They are found only inside a box or a chest, waiting malevolently for someone or something to come and open it! Related to Gremlins, they are small, mischievous humanoids, with very long arms that end in strong, claw-tipped hands. When the Beast hears a suitable victim approaching its hiding-place, it will crouch, ready to spring out and attack. The moment the lid is lifted, it will leap up and slash out violently with its claws at the nearest living thing. It will hit on a roll of 1–4 on one die, causing 4 points of STAMINA damage. Once the Chestrap Beast has appeared, it may be attacked as normal. Inside their chests there may be all sorts of treasure, for the Chestrap Beast is a great hoarder of relics stolen from past victims.

CLAWBEAST

SKILL: 9   2 Attacks
STAMINA: 14
HABITAT: Hills, Plains, Forests
NUMBER ENCOUNTERED: 1
TYPE: Monster
REACTION: Hostile
INTELLIGENCE: Low

Some species have evolved, in isolation in the wild, into savage carnivorous killing machines. Lions and sharks are prime examples; less common are the Gretch of the southern deserts, and the CLAW-BEASTS of the north. Taller than a man by almost a head, they are brutish killers, covered in long shaggy clumps of thick hair, which gives them a mottled colouring somewhere between green, grey and brown. They have four arms, instead of two, and each ends in a vicious curving hook which they use like scythes when attacking. In the wild these predators are rarely found together, for their vast appetites and prodigious hunting can clear an area of all suitable food in a few weeks. As a result, Clawbeasts are perpetually on the move, searching for fresh hunting-grounds where they can feed for a short while before migrating onwards.

It is whispered that a few of these creatures are kept by an unknown nobleman in the southlands. The evil lord allows them to roam his treasure-vaults, tossing down to them just enough food each day to stop them eating one another, but not enough to satisfy their hunger. As a result, the Clawbeasts roam far and wide through their subterranean reaches, sniffing for food as they wander.

CLONE

	Worker	Warrior
SKILL:	0	6
STAMINA:	2	5

HABITAT: Caves, Ruins, Dungeons
NUMBER ENCOUNTERED:
  Workers – 2–12
  Warriors – 1–6
TYPE: Plant/humanoid
REACTION:
  Workers – Neutral
  Warriors – Hostile
INTELLIGENCE:
  Workers – None
  Warriors – Low

Some of the favourite dishes for the lavish banquets of the Demon Princes of Hell are made from various species of giant mushroom found only on the Earthly Plane. As a result, their servants (ever anxious to please their diabolic masters) have established a number of farms in isolated underground caverns to grow the fungi. When they first came to employ workers for the farms, however, they found a slight problem. Demonic Servants were too high in the social ladder of the Abyss to work on a mushroom farm themselves, and the Demonspawn were far too chaotic – one moment they were holding a spade, the next they were a pool of gibbering slime! So instead they use CLONES, small humanoids created from the giant fungi themselves, with Workers to rear the crop and Warriors to guard the Workers.

All Clones are short, pale-skinned humanoids, with vacant eyes and no hair. The Workers are placid, brainless beings, able only to tend their fungi. If spoken to, challenged or even attacked, they will take no notice whatsoever, and just continue with their work. A single blow is enough to kill them. When they die, their bodies dissolve into different-coloured pools of water, from which a fresh mushroom will sprout after a few minutes.

The Clone Warriors are slightly taller than the Workers they guard; they dress in leather armour, and will be carrying long spears. Their large eyes are still lifeless and blank, though, which can be very disconcerting for their opponent. They will usually be found a short distance from the Workers, where they can watch both them and the surrounding area.

The Clones are controlled by some more intelligent being wearing a special magical crown, typically a Lesser Demon. The crown enables the wearer to give and receive telepathic speech to and from the Clones, though the Workers will talk only of their crops, and the Warriors of their last security patrol. The command of a fungus plantation is often given to wayward Demons as a punishment (for being too nice, washing too much – that sort of thing). In such cases, the crown can only be removed from their heads by a Greater Demon or on the being's death; once it is placed on a new head, the same will apply and the new wearer will be trapped, condemned to watch over the mushrooms for eternity.

COCKATRICE

SKILL: 7   2 Attacks
STAMINA: 7
HABITAT: Wilderness, Plains, Caves, Ruins,
   Dungeons
NUMBER ENCOUNTERED: 1
TYPE: Monster
REACTION: Hostile
INTELLIGENCE: Low

The COCKATRICE is a rare mythological beast much feared by even the bravest hero. Also known as the King of Serpents in some lands, it is a curious amalgam of a number of different creatures. It has the head and body of a large cockerel, the large leathery wings of a bat, and a long snake-like tail. It can fly short distances, but will usually strut about on the ground flapping its wings. It is carnivorous, and will fearlessly attack any large creature it encounters.

In an attack a Cockatrice will attempt to peck with its beak, which will do 2 points of damage in a successful strike. However, the beast also has poisonous breath, which will paralyse anything it comes into contact with. If the Cockatrice hits with its beak, two dice should be rolled to indicate which part of its opponent's body is affected.

Dice Roll	Area Affected	Effect
2	Brain	Death
3	Sword-arm	Must use other arm to attack – lose 4 SKILL points
4	Back	Difficult to move – lose 3 SKILL points
5	Left leg	Can only limp along – lose 2 SKILL points
6	Second arm	Cannot use arm – lose 1 SKILL point
7	None	No penalty
8	One eye	3-D vision gone – lose 1 SKILL point
9	Right leg	Can only limp along – lose 2 SKILL points
10	Both legs	Cannot move – lose 3 SKILL points
11	Both arms	Cannot use arms to fight, carry anything, etc.
12	Heart	Death

Anyone caught by the Cockatrice's breath has a chance of dodging the worst of it by a successful *Test for Luck*: the dice may then be rolled again and the adventurer may choose which of the two results to apply, the other roll being ignored.

Like the Basilisk, to which it is distantly related, the Cockatrice has a major weakness. If it catches sight of its reflection in a mirror or some other reflective surface it will die. Persuading a hungry Cockatrice to stop and look into a mirror requires its opponent to *Test for Luck* twice. If he fails on either roll, the Cockatrice may decide to attack while he is occupied, scoring an automatic hit. No one is sure why the thing can be killed in this way, but this knowledge has proved useful to a number of lucky adventurers through the years.

GIANT CRAB

	Large	Small
SKILL:	10	7
STAMINA:	11	9

HABITAT: Sea-shore
NUMBER ENCOUNTERED: 1
TYPE: Crustacean
REACTION: Unfriendly
INTELLIGENCE: Low–None

Along the coasts of Allansia and Kakhabad, and on other deserted shores, GIANT CRABS can occasionally be found. They bury themselves, until just a pair of long eyestalks poke out of a tell-tale hump in the sand near the water's edge. Should a suitable meal pass by (and they will eat almost any creature), the Crab will break free of its hiding-place, scuttle across the sand on its four pairs of spiny legs, and try to grab it in its pincers. For this first attack, the Giant Crab can add 2 to its SKILL, as it surprises its victim. After their first attack they will fight as normal, unless this first attack succeeded. In this instance, they will have caught their opponent in a pincer, and the trapped victim will have his SKILL reduced by 2, until he can kill the Giant Crab and get free.

Giant Crabs can measure anything from one to five metres across, and may stand almost as high as a man. They are typically coloured a sandy yellow-green, with a lighter underside, though colours vary from place to place. They are solitary creatures, and will only be found alone, close to the water in which they spend most of their lives.

CROCODILE

SKILL: 7   2 Attacks
STAMINA: 7
HABITAT: Rivers, Lakes, Sea
NUMBER ENCOUNTERED: 1–2
TYPE: Reptile
REACTION: Unfriendly
INTELLIGENCE: Low

CROCODILES may be found lining the banks of rivers and lakes throughout the warm southern lands, though they have been reported much further north. These huge reptiles, often as much as six metres long, are known for their voracious appetites, and they spend much of their day swimming in search of fish, or larger prey if they are lucky, visible only as a pair of eyes peeking out

above the surface. The rest of the time, they will be basking on the shore in the sun. Crocodiles may be tremendously aggressive, and are not afraid to attack men or other creatures which disturb them. They are not so skilled when fighting on land (their SKILL being reduced by 2 points), but if they can lure or drag their prey into the water to fight, they will prove deadly opponents.

CRYPT STALKER

SKILL: 8
STAMINA: 6
HABITAT: Ruins, Dungeons
NUMBER ENCOUNTERED: 1–2
TYPE: Undead
REACTION: Hostile
INTELLIGENCE: Low

There is a custom in many lands decreeing that upon the death of a nobleman or high priest, his riches are entombed with him, so his power and wealth may follow him to the afterlife. However, there is also a custom in many lands that, from the moment the tomb is sealed, all the local thieves and adventurers will form a queue to break in and steal the treasure! Hence, many tombs have been given their own unsleeping guardians, undead beings ready to surprise any potential burglar.

The CRYPT STALKER is one such deathly guard, often animated from a favoured servant of the tomb's inhabitant, and sacrificed to serve his master in death as in life. It resembles a Zombie, with lifeless, rotting skin and long, dank hair; tatters of decaying raiment may still cling to its putrid flesh. Being undead, they can only be damaged by enchanted or blessed weapons; others will appear to damage them, but will not in fact do any harm.

Holy water, blessed by a high priest, will act like a strong acid if thrown over them, doing one die of STAMINA damage. In an attack against intruders, a Crypt Stalker will strike with its bare hands and grip with unearthly strength. If it scores two successful hits in a row, it will grasp its opponent's neck and strangle him for an additional die of damage. Each Attack Round after this, the victim must strike successfully and free himself of the grip, or take the same extra damage, until one or the other is killed. Crypt Stalkers do not keep any treasure of their own, but will be guarding a very rich hoard.

CRYSTAL WARRIOR

SKILL: 11
STAMINA: 13
HABITAT: In the company of a sorcerer
NUMBER ENCOUNTERED: 1
TYPE: Magical creature
REACTION: Neutral–Unfriendly
INTELLIGENCE: Low

One of the hindrances a warlock faces in pursuing his chosen craft is the amount of time spent in tedious rituals and frustrating research, and the corresponding lack of time available for learning the arts of the warrior. Consequently, many wizards are very weak and prone to all kinds of attack. To counter this, a number of defences have been invented; one is the CRYSTAL WARRIOR.

A sorcerer first takes a large block of pure quartz and fashions it into human form with a specially treated hammer and chisel. The statue is then temporarily animated by a lengthy ritual, which bears many similarities to that used in the creation of a Golem. The resulting Crystal Warrior is then set to work, patrolling the passages and chambers of the wizard's stronghold. It can memorize the faces of two people, or remember a particular symbol; these people, or anyone bearing the symbol, will be allowed to pass. All others will be challenged and then engaged in combat. A Crystal Warrior cannot be harmed by edged weapons; an opponent must use a large blunt weapon, such as a war-hammer, or be pulverized by its crushing blows.

CYCLOPS

SKILL: 10
STAMINA: 10
HABITAT: Hills, Caves
NUMBER ENCOUNTERED: 1
TYPE: Humanoid
REACTION: Hostile
INTELLIGENCE: Average

A head higher than a man, as strong as a Hill Giant but even more aggressive, a CYCLOPS may be found at the heart of many battles. These savage humanoids, instantly recognizable from their height, muscular build and the large, single eye in the centre of their forehead, have long been shunned by civilization because of their disturbing appearance, and now begrudge the existence of all humans. As a result, they will join the armies of human-hating Orcs or Lizard Men. Rising quickly up the ranks through their prowess in battle, many become feared captains, who strike such dread into their enemies that only the bravest of heroes will face them in combat. Tales of their barbarism are legendary, but most are unfortunately true: a Cyclops's loathing for humankind knows no bounds.

When encountered away from the clamour of the battlefield, a Cyclops will usually be living a solitary existence in an isolated cave in hill country far from civilization, eating small animals which it catches and kills in its brutally strong hands. Made outcasts because of their cruel and violent natures, they will instantly attack any human they encounter, afterwards wreaking their final revenge by slowly cooking and eating the bodies.

DEATH SPIDER

SKILL: 14
STAMINA: 9
HABITAT: Demonic Plane, Dungeons, Ruins
NUMBER ENCOUNTERED: 1
TYPE: Demon
REACTION: Hostile
INTELLIGENCE: High

Some Demons pass the time by roasting the souls of the damned over steaming pits of brimstone and sulphur. Others enjoy trying to tempt holy men, as they fast in the wilderness, with the delights of being evil, just once. And some stalk the Earth as DEATH SPIDERS, luring adventurers to Hell as a spider lures a fly. These diabolic creatures appear as massive grey-black spiders, but instead of normal arachnid heads they have demonic heads, with a malevolent travesty of a human face. Almost five metres across, they lurk in dungeons and ruins, ready to trap an unwary explorer.

When encountered, they will usually be in the centre of, or at least close by, a large web. This near-invisible tangle of sticky, silver strands is the Demon's link with the Realms of the Damned, and is used to capture its victims. When it attacks, the

Death Spider tries to bite its opponent, both to inflict damage and to inject a paralysing poison. If its attack succeeds, the adventurer must *Test for Luck*. If he fails, he is paralysed by the venom, and will be dragged on to the web and bitten until he dies.

Once stuck to the web, the corpse of the dead adventurer, together with the Death Spider and its ghostly web, will start to dematerialize, and return to the Demon's plane, where the soul of the victim can be extracted at its pleasure, and tortured for the rest of eternity!

DEATH WRAITH

SKILL: 9
STAMINA: 8
HABITAT: Ruins, Dungeons
NUMBER ENCOUNTERED: 1
TYPE: Undead
REACTION: Hostile
INTELLIGENCE: Average

When a truly evil man dies, his body will pass away and crumble into dust in his crypt, but his evil will remain to haunt the area, manifesting itself as a ghostly white spirit that will prey on the living. A DEATH WRAITH will only ever be found close to the coffin containing its physical remains, for the link between the two stays strong. It will be wrapped in its funeral shroud and will appear roughly humanoid in shape, with a deathly red-eyed skull and a pair of skeletal hands poking out of the ancient cloth.

Beneath the robe, however, there is nothing, for a Death Wraith is little more than a vaporous spirit, combined with a few earthly remains. As a result, blows from normal weapons will alarmingly pass straight through it! But a weapon made of silver will hit it normally, for the metal exists both on the Earthly and the Spirit Planes. In return, the ghostly Death Wraith will attack with a very real ceremonial dagger or sword, often part of the large hoard of treasure buried with its physical form when it died many centuries before.

down with a strong fever that will confine him to his bed and gradually worsen until he is very near to death. His body will be racked with great pain as mould spores begin to burst through the skin, making him lose 2 STAMINA points an hour until he dies.

During this time, the swift ministrations of an experienced healer may be able to kill the mould and halt the spread of the disease. Certain very rare herbs are needed to effect such a cure, however, and victims often die while waiting for them to be found. Should someone die from the rotting disease, they will rise as a new Decayer in twenty-four hours' time unless the body is burnt and the ashes scattered. The new Decayer will follow the orders of the creature which first infected it, and perhaps join it on its eternal guard-duty.

DECAYER

SKILL: 7
STAMINA: 5
HABITAT: Deserts, Ruins, Dungeons
NUMBER ENCOUNTERED: 1
TYPE: Undead
REACTION: Hostile
INTELLIGENCE: Low

DECAYERS are strange, mouldering skeletons, often created as guards by evil necromancers. They appear just like animated human skeletons, wrapped up in rotting clothes. Their bones are a sickly yellow, as are their vacant eyes. The air around a Decayer hangs heavy with disease and decay. Anyone coming within three metres of such a creature must successfully *Test for Luck* or come down with a heavy fever a week or so later, which gradually turns into the rotting disease described below.

In an attack, a Decayer will use its claws, while at the same time releasing a cloud of near-invisible disease-ridden spores. Anyone actually fighting the foul being at this time will automatically be infected with a cruel rotting disease that does not manifest itself for a week or so. Until that time, the victim will be completely unaware that he has been infected. After a week, he will suddenly be struck

DEMON BAT

SKILL: 7
STAMINA: 8
HABITAT: Dungeons, Ruins, Magical Plane of Fire
NUMBER ENCOUNTERED: 1–3
TYPE: Magical creature
REACTION: Hostile
INTELLIGENCE: Average

DEMON BATS usually live on the Magical Plane of Fire, a supernatural realm which they share with Fire Elementals, Imps and Sprites. Sometimes, however, they are summoned to the Earthly Plane, by way of a lengthy arcane ritual, to serve warlocks and sorcerers as guards and assassins.

They appear as ghostly, ethereal bats, whose bodies and wings scintillate with wisps of flame. They can communicate with one another using high-pitched shrieks and squeals, but are also intelligent enough to understand their summoner's wishes, provided he stays within his protective pentagram! Demon Bats are wilful, vicious creatures, and require careful handling: only the most skilled of spell-casters can deal with them.

In an attack, Demon Bats will usually try to clasp their opponent with their claws, and deliver a massive blast of fire from their bodies. If they hit him successfully twice in a row, their next successful strike will deliver an extra 5 points of damage. Similarly, if a Demon Bat is killed while on this Earthly Plane, it will expire in a burst of flame (which will deliver a further 4 points of damage to anyone within three metres of it – *Test for Luck* to avoid), before its spirit returns to the Magical Plane to be reborn.

EARTH DEMON

SKILL: 12
STAMINA: 15
HABITAT: Hills, Plains, Forests
NUMBER ENCOUNTERED: 1
TYPE: Monster
REACTION: Hostile
INTELLIGENCE: Low

Lurking just below the surface of the ground, danger waits to surprise unwary travellers in the form of EARTH DEMONS. These enormous creatures are not true Demons, but earned their name for the ferocious and alarming way they attack. The huge beasts lie a few centimetres under the ground, listening for the heavy tread of a suitable foe. When they feel one approaching, they burst out of the ground, dripping with mud and dragging roots and bushes with them. They tower over three and a half metres tall, primitive arms and tentacles reaching out to grab and crush their opponent.

An Earth Demon's strength is drawn from the soil itself. While it is in contact with the ground, a wound against it will only cause 1 point of STA-MINA damage, instead of the usual 2. However, if the monster can somehow be separated from the source of its powers, it will be seriously wounded. After a successful strike, instead of hitting the creature its opponent can try to lift it, by rolling two dice. On the roll of a double, he has managed to lift the struggling beast off the ground, causing it immediately to suffer 6 points of STAMINA damage.

Strangely enough, these belligerent creatures do not eat their opponents. They are rumoured to be the result of a failed experiment by a foolish sorcerer. A potion was spilled on the ground, creating the first Earth Demon, and the creatures have hated all mankind ever since.

DEMONIC SERVANT

SKILL: 8
STAMINA: 7
HABITAT: Demonic Plane, Ruins, Dungeons
NUMBER ENCOUNTERED: 1–3
TYPE: Demon
REACTION: Unfriendly
INTELLIGENCE: Low

In their bizarre castles in the infernal regions of Hell, the Demon Princes are served by hordes of lesser beings, usually referred to in the grimoires dealing with such subjects as DEMONIC SER-VANTS. These strange entities act as guards, acolytes, housekeepers and even sacrifices when called upon! The Servants appear as animated skeletons, clothed in loose black robes similar to monks' habits. They have sparkling red eyes, which glow when they are under the direct control of a higher being.

Demonic Servants are 'recruited' from the fresh souls of those who have served the Demon Princes during their earthly lives. Most are willing to spend the rest of eternity mindlessly at the constant beck and call of the Princes, but a few require persuading, usually by a brief exposure to the treatment normally reserved for sinners! The Servants are not too intelligent, and have no emotions or desires; they are dedicated only to the needs of their masters. They cannot speak, but communicate with their masters and one another via a form of stilted telepathy, in phrases like, 'He wants guard – we must do.' Whenever a Demon Prince visits the Earthly Plane, it will usually be accompanied by a small retinue of Servants, who will remain close at hand to attend to any of its needs. If involved in combat, a Demonic Servant will use its bare hands and quite unearthly strength, even against steel. If a Servant takes two blows in succession without itself striking, the spell animating its body will be broken, and it will collapse back into a pile of mouldering bones.

DEMONSPAWN

SKILL: 6
STAMINA: 6
HABITAT: Demonic Plane, Ruins, Dungeons
NUMBER ENCOUNTERED: 2–7 (1 die plus 1)
TYPE: Demon
REACTION: Hostile
INTELLIGENCE: Low

Writhing in the ectoplasm that gathers in fetid pools scattered here and there across the endless wastes of Hell, unclaimed souls wait to be assigned a position. Some ardent worshippers are chosen to become Demonic Servants; others are sacrificed straight away in horrific magical rites by the Demons. Most, though, join the ranks of the DEMONSPAWN – noxious, half-witted beings that serve as the rank and file in the Legions of Hell.

The forms that Demonspawn take are varied and erratic, depending solely upon the whims and imaginative powers of the Demon which animated them from the slime. Most take a vaguely human-oid shape, though they are often lumpy and malformed. Some are large and blubbery, others thin and leathery; all drip foul slime and reek of sulphur and the grave. Their colouring is equally varied, but whatever the hues, they are always combined in a way that repulses the eye and nauseates the stomach. Some Demonspawn have multiple heads or arms; others have malformed limbs, or those of other creatures; still others have no recognizable shape at all. All possibilities are present, but all appear in such an unholy, wholly evil way that most creatures who side with Good against Chaos will attack them desperately on encountering them. A typical Demonspawn will stand somewhat over a metre high, but its size can vary tremendously, just like everything else. Most will be equipped with horns, tusks, claws or teeth, with which they can be surprisingly adept at stabbing, gouging, rending or biting. On the other hand, Demonspawn can only be harmed by magi-cal weapons. Other implements will appear to injure them, but the wounds will close up again and severed parts will reattach themselves!

Demonspawn do not have eyes; instead, their place is taken by a pair of large sensory pits, like shadowy hollows, with which the vile creatures can dimly perceive the aura of life surrounding other beings. Their lack of eyes has added much weight to the widespread belief among earthly scholars that the souls of living creatures are contained in the eyes (a belief hotly disputed by most blind sages).

Demonspawn are usually confined to their home planes, where they are often enlisted to fight in the many civil wars which occur between the Demons. Occasionally, though, they can be found on Earth, in centres of great evil, where they have been summoned along with their diabolic masters. Demonspawn rarely live more than a few years before their bodies become uninhabitable. When they 'die', their bodies shrivel, hissing and steam-ing, until they are nothing but a pool of rank-smelling slime.

DEVLIN

SKILL: 10
STAMINA: 0 (see below)
HABITAT: Magical Plane of Fire
NUMBER ENCOUNTERED: 1
TYPE: Magical creature
REACTION: Hostile
INTELLIGENCE: Low

On the Magical Plane of Fire there are many spirit creatures that can be summoned to the Earthly Plane to serve a clever sorcerer. The DEVLINS are one such race, related to the larger Fire Elementals and the smaller Fire Sprites. They appear as roughly humanoid beings, as tall as a Dwarf, but made up of a myriad tongues of fire. Their summoning can be long and complicated, for an unprotected warlock can easily fall victim to the creatures. Some, however, have found a way of creating a partial ritual, which needs only one simple action – such as the speaking of a command or the tossing of dust on a fire – to bring a Devlin hastening to this plane to do their will.

Devlins can be very frightening and dangerous creatures, since they cannot be harmed by earthly weapons, but they can singe away 2 points of damage if they win an attack. The only sure way of banishing a Devlin is to douse it with liquid and extinguish it completely. Such an action will require a large container of water or another liquid, and a *Test for Luck*. If the throw is successful, there will be a short stifled scream as the water douses the fire, and the spirit of the Devlin will be sent back to the Magical Plane of Fire in extreme agony.

DINOSAUR

All DINOSAURS are giant, leathery-skinned reptiles, noted mostly for their stupidity and their voracious appetites. They are found in many wild areas across the world, but they prefer warmer climes, for they are cold-blooded creatures. The land-based dinosaurs will not usually be encountered near settled areas, where they would be hunted out of existence. Various of the lizard races, especially Lizard Men, have been able to rear several types from eggs, keeping them as pets and steeds until they become too large and unmanageable.

There are many different types of Dinosaur to be found in various parts of the world. Detailed below are examples of the five main types, on which other specific creatures can be based.

BRONTOSAURUS

	Adult	Young	
SKILL:	12	8	4 Attacks
STAMINA:	25	18	

HABITAT: Marshes, Lakes, Jungles, Wilderness
NUMBER ENCOUNTERED: 1–3
TYPE: Reptile
REACTION: Neutral
INTELLIGENCE: Low

Upwards of twenty metres long and weighing seventy tonnes when fully grown, these monstrosities are thankfully plant-eaters. Their grey bodies are large and flabby, and supported on four stumpy legs. At one end a very long, thin tail helps them keep their balance; at the other end a neck, very similar to its tail, extends for many metres before reaching its head. They spend most of their time immersed in water or mud which helps them support their vast bulk. Their necks stretch out over the land to pluck fruit, leaves and even whole branches from trees and bushes. If encountered on land, it is likely that they will not notice a smaller creature and may step on it, with fatal results. They are docile beasts and will not attack another creature, even if they are being attacked. Finding the right place to hit a Brontosaurus so that the blow actually does some damage, however, is very hard, and hence its high SKILL score. Most Brontosauruses will be adults; if three or more are encountered, two will be fully grown and the others will be younger creatures.

PLESIOSAURUS

SKILL: 9   3 Attacks
STAMINA: 22
HABITAT: Sea, Lakes
NUMBER ENCOUNTERED: 1
TYPE: Reptile
REACTION: Hostile
INTELLIGENCE: Low

The largest of the sea-dwelling Dinosaurs is the PLESIOSAURUS, a gigantic beast with a rounded body from which a thin neck supports a snake-like head. Known to grow up to fifteen metres long, they propel their huge blue-green bodies through the oceans with gigantic flippers at great speed, searching for food. They have been known to attack fishing-boats and small ships, smashing the hull and then picking off the drowning men one by one. More usually they eat fish, dolphins and even small whales, when they can find them.

PTERODACTYL
SKILL: 7
STAMINA: 9
HABITAT: Wilderness, Hills, Forests, Jungles
NUMBER ENCOUNTERED: 1–2
TYPE: Reptile
REACTION: Hostile
INTELLIGENCE: Low

PTERODACTYLS are large and repulsive flying Dinosaurs. They are like scrawny lizards, with a pair of leathery wings stretched out from their elongated forelegs to their ankles, giving them a wingspan approaching five metres. They are carnivores, living mostly on small animals and fish, and have become skilled at swooping down and grabbing their prey in their long jaws, before swallowing them in a single gulp. When faced with larger opponents, however, they will try to bite them, before carrying their corpses off to their nest to tear them up and eat them.

STYRACOSAURUS

	Adult	Young	
SKILL:	12	11	3 Attacks
STAMINA:	18	10	

HABITAT: Plains, Wilderness, Jungles
NUMBER ENCOUNTERED: 1
TYPE: Reptile
REACTION: Hostile
INTELLIGENCE: Low

Though they live solely on plants, these Dinosaurs are aggressive, violent beasts that will charge, head down, at anything that appears to threaten them. STYRACOSAURUSES are large, fat, four-legged creatures, growing up to six metres long and two metres high. Their grey hides are thick with folds of leathery skin, and their large heads have long horns and a bony collar for further protection. Any hit on a Styracosaurus will only cause it 1 point of damage, because of the thickness of its hide. Young Styracosauruses can sometimes be trained, if domesticated early enough, and can carry riders into battle. They are very temperamental beasts, though, and will not always do as they are told, preferring to throw off their rider and charge headlong away from the battle.

TYRANNOSAURUS REX

	Adult	Young	
SKILL:	15	12	3 Attacks
STAMINA:	20	12	

HABITAT: Jungles, Wilderness
NUMBER ENCOUNTERED: 1
TYPE: Reptile
REACTION: Hostile
INTELLIGENCE: Low

The king of all the Dinosaurs, these terrible monsters can grow to a height of seven metres and measure sixteen metres from snout to tail. They stand on two legs, balance by their long tails and, despite their size, can outrun most creatures. Their heads can be as much as two metres long; their mouths are crammed with dagger-sized teeth. They are the most aggressive beasts ever to stalk the world, and will attack any creature. They are naturally solitary, for a hungry TYRANNOSAURUS can clear an area of game in the space of a few days before being forced to move on. Their teeth, claws and bulk, and the sheer ferocity of their attacks, mean that they will cause 4 points of damage in a successful strike, rather than the usual 2 points.

Younger Tyrannosauruses are perfect replicas of their parents, stand three metres tall at birth and grow rapidly. The eggs of these Dinosaurs can fetch up to 1,000 Gold Pieces if they contain live young. Getting them to a potential buyer can be something of a struggle, however, as they can be as much as two metres across and weigh 250 kilograms!

DOG

	Death Dog	Wolf Dog	Wild Dog
SKILL:	9	7	4
STAMINA:	10	6	4
HABITAT:			

   Death/Wolf Dog – Towns, Ruins, anywhere master is
   Wild Dog – Plains, Wilderness
NUMBER ENCOUNTERED: 1–3
TYPE: Animal
REACTION: Neutral–Hostile
INTELLIGENCE: Average–Low

DOGS are very useful animals, for they can be tamed fairly easily and trained for all kinds of tasks, including guarding, hunting and fighting. There are a number of different species, each ideal for a specific purpose. DEATH DOGS, also known as Moon Dogs after their terrifying habit of baying at a full moon, are the most savage of all dogs. Huge, midnight-black beasts the size of a fully grown Wolf, they are truly vicious creatures with fangs more suited to a beast four times their size. They are very cunning, and can be sent to hunt down and kill specific enemies. They are sometimes even used in battle, equipped with spiked collars and sent into the fray to kill horses and their riders. They are difficult creatures to handle, as their violent instincts tend to overwhelm their loyalty to their masters in the end, and they may turn on them unless kept very well fed.

The most common domesticated hounds are WOLF DOGS. They grow up to about a metre long, and are coloured brown or black. Some types can be trained as guard-dogs, others as hounds for hunting game such as foxes, deer and boar. Once trained they are very obedient, and will serve their masters faithfully. If their master is threatened they need no command to attack with their sharp teeth. Surprisingly strong and savage when roused, their training keeps them far more controllable than Death Dogs.

Roaming the open plains in small packs, WILD DOGS are thin, scrawny beasts, who are ravenously hungry nearly all the time. They can grow up to about a metre in length, and are typically coloured sandy-brown to black, with lighter markings. A pack will usually be led by a stronger Dog, with SKILL 6, STAMINA 5; if this beast is killed, the rest of the pack will flee in disarray and confusion.

from its ragged tresses. The creatures dress in armour welded from large metal plates and decorated with spikes and studs, which they use as offensive weapons, impaling their enemies on them in the press of battle. Like the Doragar themselves, their weapons are large and cruel, made without thought for the grace and skill of fighting.

DORAGAR

SKILL: 9
STAMINA: 10
HABITAT: Caves, Dungeons, Ruins
NUMBER ENCOUNTERED: 1–6
TYPE: Humanoid
REACTION: Hostile
INTELLIGENCE: Low

In the fetid darkness deep underground, evil creatures mine ore and beat metal on anvils, ever preparing for war. Orcs, Ogres and Trolls hone their weapons, repair their chainmail and shields, and ready the DORAGAR with battle-songs and strong liquor. Doragar are the shock troops of the forces of Chaos, berserk warriors which lead the howling rabble into battle. The result of careful interbreeding between Orcs and Trolls, they are brutish, ignorant beings, useful only for wielding a pick or an axe. In rare times of peace, they are set to work in the mines, where their strong bodies enable them to work twice as fast as their Orc cousins. When the tribes gather to raid the rich cities of men, Doragar are equipped with bizarrely spiked armour and huge serrated weapons, and pushed into the front lines.

The brutes stand about two metres tall, and are almost as wide. Their bodies are leathery and muscular, and their strength is prodigious. Their heads are very much like those of Orcs or Trolls, with large ragged ears and tusk-like teeth. Their hair, however, is long and luxuriant, more of a mane than a growth. Doragar are immensely proud of their rather incongruous hair, plaiting it endlessly and hanging bones and stolen trinkets

DRACON

SKILL: 9   2 Attacks
STAMINA: 14
HABITAT: Hills, Caves, Ruins
NUMBER ENCOUNTERED: 1–2
TYPE: Monster
REACTION: Neutral–Unfriendly
INTELLIGENCE: Average

In the time of legends, Rogaar the Lord of Lions took as his mate a beautiful Golden Dragon called Chrysolla. Their offspring were numerous, and still exist today – the DRACONS. The creatures are large, almost six metres long and standing as tall as a man. They have the bodies of enormous lions, with huge clawed feet. Their heads are large and leonine, with the exquisite eyes and ferocious teeth of a dragon. Their manes shimmer like a shower of molten gold, and their bodies are sleek and powerful. They can fly short distances with the help of the pair of small wings which sprout from their shoulders.

Dracons are rarely seen by men, as they prefer to dwell in desolate, forgotten places – old ruins, abandoned caves and the like. They are proud, rather haughty beasts, as befits their heritage, and are only too willing to expound all the intricate details of their distant family trees to anyone willing to listen to them. They are very fastidious about good manners, and can quicky become irate if their guests turn out to be rude and boorish in their behaviour. In an attack they will either slash with their claws or bite with their oversized teeth. Throughout a fight, they will mock their opponents, deriding their skill, abusing their parents and family, and cursing any successful blows. Should they be overwhelmed, they will attempt to escape rather than die. If flight proves impossible, they may offer some items from their large but well-hidden treasure-hoards in return for their lives. An honourable adventurer can often bargain his way to a choice treasure; a greedy or dishonest man may be passed a cursed item for his rudeness: Dracons are obsessed with manners, in even the most desperate circumstances.

DRAGON

Of all the frightful, terrifying and downright awesome beings that stalk the earth, none are as powerful as the DRAGONS. Some say the race of Dragonkind is as old as time itself; there were certainly Dragons around to be recorded in the first histories of mankind. In the past the old civilizations were great allies of the Dragons, and they shared much knowledge. Young Dragons allowed themselves to be ridden by humans, even in battle, where their combined powers helped drive the armies of Chaos and Evil back under the ground.

Nowadays the old Dragons hide themselves away,

sleeping out the millennia until civilization needs them again. Younger Dragons still stalk the earth, but many are evil creatures, concerned only with acquiring gold and treasure. In some of the newer kingdoms there are people who have never seen a Dragon, for they are now very rare creatures.

Dragons are the noblest of all reptilian races, gigantic winged creatures with long necks and tails. There are many sub-species, each with its own skin colour and other individual features. All Dragons can fly, and most can speak a wide variety of human and animal languages. Dragons are able to spit fire, acid or ice from their mouths. They also have claws and fangs; even without their fatal breath they would be more than a match for the strongest of opponents. They come in different sizes and strengths, according to their age. Dragons seem to be all but immortal, and they mature only very slowly. Dragons are called young between the time they burst out of the egg and reach one hundred years of age, by which time they may have grown up to twelve metres long. They are impetuous, as Dragons go, and may be encountered in partnership with a powerful human such as a sorcerer or evil leader who can provide both protection and regular food. Young Dragons do not know much of magic or books, as they are far too busy acquiring treasure to learn from wizards or converse with sages.

Adult Dragons are aged between one hundred and five hundred years old, and can grow up to about twenty-five metres in length. There are very few adults known to mankind, for they are very rare and spend much of their time sleeping on their vast hoards in cavernous halls deep below a mountain or castle.

Old Dragons have not been seen by anyone for many hundreds of years, and it is thought they may have left this earth to live on the Magical Planes in peace. For this reason there are no details of them in the following descriptions; they will never be encountered by adventurers on the Earthly Plane.

The skin of a Dragon will easily fetch 50 Gold Pieces a metre in a large trading city, where it can be used to make superb armour. Actually acquiring the skin of a Dragon is another matter.

BLACK DRAGON

	Adult	Young	
SKILL:	16	14	4 Attacks
STAMINA:	30	20	

HABITAT: *Hills, Wilderness, Caves, Ruins*
NUMBER ENCOUNTERED: 1
TYPE: *Monster*
REACTION: *Hostile*
INTELLIGENCE: *High*

BLACK DRAGONS are usually encountered in rough, hilly terrain, where they may be preying upon villages for their livestock or people. Both young and adult Black Dragons make their lairs in caverns, to which they will return after a day's hunting. Younger creatures will have only a small, cramped cave, but an adult may occupy a vast cavern complex, housing a tribe of Goblins or Orcs as well as various other monsters, with several secret entrances for when danger threatens.

A Black Dragon's breath is unusual in that instead of the typical jet of flame, it can create a huge stinking cloud of poisonous gas. Young creatures can create one up to three metres in diameter, an adult twice that. Anyone caught within the cloud must successfully *Test for Luck* or lose 4 STAMINA points. A successful LUCK roll means they only take a single point of damage. A young Black Dragon can produce such a cloud only once every six Attack Rounds; an adult once every four rounds.

GOLD DRAGON

	Adult	Young	
SKILL:	18	16	4 Attacks
STAMINA:	40	25	

HABITAT: *Deserts, Mountains, Wilderness*
NUMBER ENCOUNTERED: *1*
TYPE: *Monster*
REACTION: *Neutral*
INTELLIGENCE: *High*

The largest and noblest of all their race, GOLD DRAGONS are only rarely encountered by humans. They prefer to inhabit large towers or castles in the middle of deserts or at the top of mountains, well removed from most other creatures. They are better disposed towards humans than other Dragons, though they cannot understand that their short life-span makes them seem impatient and rude. Gold Dragons tend to be especially friendly with sages and sorcerers, who sometimes visit them with questions on ancient history or magic. The Dragons dislike the more primitive and violent humanoid races, though, and will normally attack them on sight.

Gold Dragons can breathe a wide jet of flame every other Attack Round. This is broad enough to hit two opponents, and requires a *Test for Luck* to avoid it. It will scorch away 2 STAMINA points if it hits (an adult's will cause 4 points of damage). Creatures aged more than about seventy years may also have magical spells to back up their claws and teeth; they are particularly fond of illusions and tricks. The armoured hide of a Gold Dragon is very tough, and blows against it will only cause 1 point of damage to the huge creature.

GREEN DRAGON

	Adult	Young	
SKILL:	15	13	4 Attacks
STAMINA:	26	18	

HABITAT: *Forests, Jungles, Caves, Ruins*
NUMBER ENCOUNTERED: *1*
TYPE: *Monster*
REACTION: *Unfriendly*
INTELLIGENCE: *High*

A young GREEN DRAGON may be encountered amid the tangles at the centre of a large forest, where it will make its lair in an old ruin or a shallow cave in a hillside. An adult creature will only be encountered deep in a tropical jungle, well away from any settlements, where it can enjoy being the largest and most voracious predator in the region. Green Dragons are natural hunters, both quick and cunning, and make fearsome opponents. In combat they can breathe out a thin stream of fire once every three Attack Rounds. If their opponent fails to roll his current SKILL or under on two dice, he will be burnt for 2 STAMINA points of damage (4 points from an adult creature).

RED DRAGON

	Adult	Young	
SKILL:	14	11	3 Attacks
STAMINA:	23	14	

HABITAT: *Hills, Wilderness, Caves, Dungeons*
NUMBER ENCOUNTERED: *1*
TYPE: *Monster*
REACTION: *Hostile*
INTELLIGENCE: *High*

RED DRAGONS are hoarders who relish collecting coins, jewels and all other valuable items. When encountered, a Red Dragon will usually be in its cavern, sprawled across the top of a large pile of treasure. Red Dragons are automatically suspicious of anyone they encounter, believing them to be thieves intent on stealing their treasure, and will attack them immediately. They can shoot fire-balls from their mouths, which they send roaring through the air to explode on their target. These can be avoided by a successful *Test for Luck*; if they hit they will cause 2 STAMINA points of damage (4 from an adult Red Dragon). The creatures can produce one of these every other round, and can shoot them up to twenty-five metres with surprising accuracy.

SILVER DRAGON

	Adult	Young	
SKILL:	17	15	4 Attacks
STAMINA:	30	22	

HABITAT: *Wilderness, Ice*
NUMBER ENCOUNTERED: *1*
TYPE: *Monster*
REACTION: *Unfriendly–Hostile*
INTELLIGENCE: *High*

SILVER DRAGONS have long been the arch-enemies of their Gold cousins, for they are very jealous of their status among the rest of Dragon-kind. They seem to be perpetually plotting against their noble relations, though events rarely get violent. Silver Dragons live in desolate areas away from other creatures, for they can be bad-tempered and aggressive.

In an attack a Silver Dragon can shoot out a chilling sheet of cold that is wide enough to hit two opponents at once. Unless its targets can roll their current SKILL score or less on two dice, they will lose 2 STAMINA points (4 from an adult Dragon). The creatures can breathe cold once every three Attack Rounds. Silver Dragons fear fire, though, and would rather give away part of their vast treasure-hoard than face several creatures wielding it against them.

WHITE DRAGON

	Adult	Young	
SKILL:	15	12	3 Attacks
STAMINA:	22	14	

HABITAT: *Ice, Wilderness, Caves*
NUMBER ENCOUNTERED: *1*
TYPE: *Monster*
REACTION: *Hostile*
INTELLIGENCE: *High*

Of all the desolate, inhospitable places that Dragons inhabit, nowhere is worse than that of the WHITE DRAGONS. They can only survive in sub-zero temperatures, so they will only ever be encountered amid the snow and ice of the extreme northern lands, beyond the Icefinger Mountains. They dwell in vast caves or castles carved from the ice itself. They are the most unpredictable of all Dragons, and will normally eat any being they come across. In keeping with its frigid home, a White Dragon can breathe out a stream of ice that will freeze its opponent. This will hit its target on a roll of 1 or 2 on one die, causing an extra 3 points of damage (5 if the Dragon is an adult). A White Dragon will not eat its dead prey straight away. Sometimes, especially when the long northern winter draws near, they will leave the bodies inside large blocks of ice, to keep until other food is scarce, when they will claw them out and eat them!

GIANT DRAGONFLY

SKILL: *8*
STAMINA: *4*
HABITAT: *Marshes, Rivers*
NUMBER ENCOUNTERED: *1–3*
TYPE: *Insect*
REACTION: *Unfriendly*
INTELLIGENCE: *Low*

Skimming at high speed just above the reeds on the hunt for a suitable meal, GIANT DRAGONFLIES are dazzling but dangerous creatures. They prey on any warm-blooded creatures they can catch, even men, swooping down and biting with their large mandibles. A Giant Dragonfly will hover threateningly over a potential victim for a long while before striking, its delicate wings a blur of movement as it hangs motionless. Then they will drop on to their prey, grab and restrain it with their legs, and bite deeply. The skin of a Giant Dragonfly is exquisitely patterned and coloured, and can fetch a good price from a high-class tailor in a large city, by whom it is used to make fine cloaks or tunics for princes and noblemen.

DRIPPER PLANT

SKILL: *0 (see below)*
STAMINA: *10*
HABITAT: *Forests, Ruins, Hills*
NUMBER ENCOUNTERED: *1–2*
TYPE: *Plant*
REACTION: *Neutral*
INTELLIGENCE: *None*

The DRIPPER PLANT (or Death Dripper, as forest lore sometimes has it) is a very strange carnivorous shrub, which ensnares its food with deadly poison. Standing about three metres tall, the plant has a wide, thick-barked trunk, which only branches into palm-like fronds at the top. Scattered among the leaves are star-shaped yellow flowers which bloom all year round. These flowers hang out over the mat of spindly roots that gather around the base of the plant. Should any creature disturb these roots, the flowers will release a glutinous, honey-like poison. The fluid will hit its intended victims unless they *Test for Luck* successfully. Otherwise, the fast-acting contact poison will kill them within a few agonizing moments. A victim's body will be encircled by the roots, which break up the plant's food so that it can decompose and be ingested quickly. Dripper Plants can sometimes be spotted by tell-tale piles of metal items gathered around their bases; many a victim has been caught in a shower of deadly poison while trying to recover treasure from among the hair-trigger roots. It is thought that Dripper Plants may be somehow related to Stranglebush, another carnivorous trapper plant.

DWARF

SKILL: 7
STAMINA: 7
HABITAT: Hills, Mountains, Plains, Towns, Caves, Dungeons
NUMBER ENCOUNTERED: 1–6
TYPE: Humanoid
REACTION: Friendly–Unfriendly
INTELLIGENCE: High

There are some races which were roaming the earth when man was still swinging about in trees. Nowadays most of them, especially Elves, keep out of men's affairs as much as they are able. The DWARFS, however, have long learnt to live alongside the younger race, who recognize them as doughty warriors and skilled craftsmen. The town of Stonebridge on the Red River is almost exclusively inhabited by Dwarfs, but in many other settlements they live alongside men.

A typical Dwarf stands only about a metre tall, yet looks a good deal older than the humans who tower over him. Their faces are wrinkled and weather-beaten, usually somewhere between ruddy-pink and brown. Their fashion is for long bushy beards, some of which are so long they need to be plaited and wrapped around their waists like belts. Their clothes are made from fine worked leather, though these will usually be covered with light jerkins of

strong mail. Their favourite weapons are battle-axes, war-hammers and other hewing weapons, for they are skilled at mining and stone-working as well as fighting.

Dwarfs are fond of ale, pipe tobacco and a good tale of heroic deeds. They are not so fond of over-hasty people, preferring to take life steadily and calmly. Sometimes quick of anger if slighted by an ill-mannered human, they are not averse to teaching some manners. They can be very honourable beings, however, and they appreciate bravery and good fighting. They despise Orcs, Goblins and other cruel cowardly beings, and stories of their interminable wars deep under the earth are frequent. Above all, Dwarfs love precious jewels and metals, and they spend much of their time mining them from the earth before jealously hoarding them away from potential thieves.

EAGLE

	Eagle	Goldcrest Eagle	Giant Eagle
SKILL:	4	7	6
STAMINA:	5	6	11

HABITAT: Mountains, Hills, Wilderness
NUMBER ENCOUNTERED: 1–2
TYPE: Bird
REACTION: Neutral–Unfriendly
INTELLIGENCE: Low

EAGLES may be encountered in rocky, mountainous areas across the whole of Allansia and beyond, where they make their nests at the top of high trees or perched on sheer cliffs. They are predatory birds, living on rabbits, fish, rats and other small creatures, though stories abound of Eagles taking sheep and even children. Usually they will not attack humans unless they appear to be threatening the Eagle's nest or chicks. Their first attack will be a great swooping dive, which will add 3 points to their SKILL as they come screeching down, talons outstretched. After this first swoop their SKILL will revert to normal.

Eagles are fairly difficult to train, even for hunting, for they are the wildest of all the birds of prey.

Nevertheless, their eggs may fetch as much as 200 Gold Pieces each from a nobleman or bird-trainer.

Most common species of Eagle will conform to the general notes above, but there are a couple of extraordinary types that require further explanation. GOLDCREST EAGLES are found only in the hills of Analand in southern Kakhabad. They are larger than most Eagles, with a wingspan of well over three metres, and have a brilliant patch of gold on their heads which gives them their name. Unlike most species, they have been extensively trained for many centuries by the people of Analand, and are now reared in captivity. They are sometimes used for fighting and hunting, but they are most effective as messengers, carrying urgent news and orders as fast as the wind, and hidden from the eyes of enemies under a cloak of invisibility. For Goldcrest Eagles need only concentrate and they will disappear, to fly on their mission in safety. If they ever need to fight, however, they will lose their concentration and become visible, but the huge birds have been trained well and they are skilful fighters.

GIANT EAGLES are only ever found in the most desolate places, well away from humans who would hunt and kill them, and steal their eggs and young to tame. They stand as tall as a man, with a wingspan approaching eight metres when fully outstretched, and their talons are like curved daggers. They live on any creatures they can catch, and are not averse to attacking humans. Like their smaller cousins, they will initially attack in a powerful dive. If a Giant Eagle scores two hits in succession, it will grasp its prey in its talons and fly off back to its huge nest high in the mountains, with a tasty morsel for its young.

All EELS are long and extremely thin in proportion to their length; they may be found in a variety of places from open sea to swamp. Most are harmless, but a few species can prove dangerous to an adventurer.

BLOOD EELS grow up to a metre long, and live in fresh water. They are savage predators, occasionally even attacking and killing pike, with which they have a great rivalry for prey. They have also been known to attack humans wading or swimming in their river. They will glide silently up to their prey and bite with needle-like teeth, automatically doing 2 points of damage. After their first attack they can be fought normally, but their opponent will have his SKILL temporarily reduced by 2 points for trying to fight in the water.

ELECTRIC EELS are only found in warm coastal waters. They are fairly small, and rarely grow to more than half a metre long. They have developed the ability to emit a strong burst of electricity, which is usually enough to stun or kill the small fish they live on. The charge can be emitted only twice a day before it is depleted, each burst doing 4 points of damage. They can also attack normally, though if their electricity is not enough to kill potential prey, they may decide to leave it well alone!

Most dangerous of all are GIANT EELS, as they can grow up to eight metres long and thirty centimetres thick. They are very strong and well equipped for hunting – their teeth are like small daggers – and are capable of catching and killing crocodiles and other large creatures. If an adventurer is attacked by a Giant Eel in water more than a metre deep, he must defeat the monster in less Attack Rounds than his current SKILL score or he will be entangled in its crushing coils and drowned.

EEL

	Blood Eel	Electric Eel	Giant Eel
SKILL:	5	6	8
STAMINA:	4	4	8

HABITAT: Rivers, Marshes, Sea
NUMBER ENCOUNTERED: 1–2
TYPE: Fish
REACTION: Unfriendly
INTELLIGENCE: Low

ELEMENTAL

ELEMENTALS are arcane magical beings, made up of concentrations of the primary elements – Air, Earth, Fire and Water. They normally dwell on their appropriate Magical Plane, but can be conjured to the Earthly Plane to serve powerful magicians. Some Elementals actually live on this plane, in areas where the element is concentrated – deep in the oceans, at the heart of volcanoes and so on.

Conjuring an Elemental is a strenuous and extremely hazardous operation, usually attempted by only the most powerful wizards. Elementals resent being summoned, and may attack their conjurer unless they can concentrate on controlling the creature. Warding devices such as pentagrams and chalk circles will not hold back the might of a raging being of pure energy for long!

Some especially careful warlocks have managed to create partial summoning spells, which they bind into elaborate scrolls or runes. In these devices, the ritual for summoning the Elemental is unfinished, needing only a magical command to be completed and bring the creature to earth. Elementals summoned in this way can sometimes be banished again by repeating the command, though this does not always work – as some have found out to their cost. The four types of Elemental are detailed below.

AIR ELEMENTAL

SKILL: 15   2 Attacks
STAMINA: 20
HABITAT: Magical Plane of Air, at the heart of a
    hurricane
NUMBER ENCOUNTERED: 1
TYPE: Magical creature
REACTION: Neutral–Unfriendly
INTELLIGENCE: Low

The force of a raging AIR ELEMENTAL is enough to tear the roof off a palace, flatten a whole village, or lift a man and throw him many metres into the air. When one is summoned, it appears as a whirlwind of air, spinning and dancing at high speed. The air around the creature howls as the raging wind sucks up rocks, stones and other small items, and spits them out into the air.

Like all Elementals, they can only be hit by enchanted weapons. Trying to stand up to an angry Air Elemental, however, requires great strength. Should anyone try to withstand the raging blast, he must *Test for Luck*. If unsuccessful, he will be knocked flying, and lose 1 SKILL point and a die of STAMINA damage. If he maintains his footing with a successful throw, he will still lose 2 STAMINA points, but will be able to keep standing long enough to attempt two strikes, before having to *Test for Luck* again. Air Elementals are immensely strong and can rarely be killed. Worse still, when they die, their spirits simply return to their home plane to recuperate and heal. A banished Air Elemental cannot be recalled to earth for sixty-six days.

EARTH ELEMENTAL

SKILL: 18   2 Attacks
STAMINA: 22
HABITAT: Magical Plane of Earth, deep underground
NUMBER ENCOUNTERED: 1
TYPE: Magical creature
REACTION: Hostile
INTELLIGENCE: Low

EARTH ELEMENTALS are the strongest and most evil of all the Elementals. They are very hard to summon and control, so they are rarely found on the Earthly Plane in the service of a wizard. Should they be encountered at all, it will usually be deep underground or high among the rocky peaks of the mountains. They appear as massive stone humanoids, covered with rocky hides. It is said that in the old days extremely adept sorcerers managed to imprison some Earth Elementals inside large masses of rock, to stop them causing earthquakes and landslides, and generally wreaking havoc around the countryside.

Freeing an Earth Elemental is extremely stupid,

and will lose the fool who does so one die of LUCK points. Actually attempting to fight an Earth Elemental is more foolish still: such a fight is virtually impossible to win! Their prodigious strength is legendary; their blows will do 4 points of damage. Worse still, the creatures can only be damaged with magical weapons, and their tough skins reduce any injury against them to only 1 point. Should an Earth Elemental actually be killed, its spirit will return to its home plane, and can never be summoned again.

FIRE ELEMENTAL

SKILL: 14   2 Attacks
STAMINA: 18
HABITAT: Magical Plane of Fire, inside volcanoes
NUMBER ENCOUNTERED: 1
TYPE: Magical creature
REACTION: Neutral
INTELLIGENCE: Average

FIRE ELEMENTALS are the most common of all these magical creatures. They are also the smallest and weakest of the four types, and are summoned and controlled more easily. Fire Elementals typically appear as vaguely humanoid figures, as tall as a man, composed solely of flames. They are far more intelligent than their fellow beings, and are more willing to be summoned to Earth, where they can add to their knowledge.

These beings can, as usual, only be hit by magical weapons. The heat of their flames will melt most things, even metals, which makes combat extremely difficult. After two successful strikes on a Fire Elemental, even an enchanted blade will be ruined. They are so hot that water thrown over them will immediately evaporate. When faced with an angry Fire Elemental, it is very important to know the command word to banish the creature home, from where it cannot be summoned for forty days.

WATER ELEMENTAL
SKILL: 16
STAMINA: 21
HABITAT: Magical Plane of Water, the deepest oceans
NUMBER ENCOUNTERED: 1
TYPE: Magical creature
REACTION: Unfriendly
INTELLIGENCE: Low

WATER ELEMENTALS are only ever encountered at sea; like all such beings, they cannot survive away from their native environment. They can be very dangerous to men and boats alike. Water Elementals are rarely summoned to this plane, and are consequently encountered very infrequently; some do dwell in the seas and oceans of the world, manifesting in a roughly humanoid form in the hearts of whirlpools and typhoons. Because of their liquid nature, they cannot be damaged by weapons at all – blades and missiles pass straight through! They are destructive beings, but prefer to smash boats and leave their occupants to drown in the swirling eddies of a whirlpool. Legend speaks of a particularly fortunate adventurer who apparently managed to trap a Water Elemental in a magical Pouch of Unlimited Contents: if the story is true, he must have been the luckiest man alive!

ELF

ELVES walked the lands while humans still lived in caves and trees, for they are a very ancient race. These tall humanoids live about twice as long as humans, whom they tend to look down on as children. All Elves are thin beings, with large ears and slanting eyes. They seem more graceful than humans, and far more intelligent somehow. They are fearless warriors, particularly expert with long-bows. There are a number of different Elven races, each sharing a common heritage, but very different from the others.

BLACK ELF
SKILL: 7
STAMINA: 6
HABITAT: Plains, Wilderness, Towns
NUMBER ENCOUNTERED: 1–6
TYPE: Humanoid
REACTION: Neutral–Unfriendly
INTELLIGENCE: High

BLACK ELVES were originally renegades from the evil kingdoms of the Dark Elves, to whom they are related. They abandoned the forests with them, and helped build their underground kingdoms, but grew more and more horrified as the Dark Elves dabbled in fearful magic and demonism. So they fled the cavern cities and settled in isolated areas away from other Elven races, where they now live squalid lives alongside Orcs, Goblins and other inhuman races.

Like all Elves they are thin and tall. Their skin is somewhere between grey and black in colour, their slanted eyes yellow and catlike. They dress in shabby clothes of outlandish design, and some-times decorate themselves in a similar fashion, with bizarrely cropped hair and painted patterns on their faces. Their favourite weapons are longbows (with a 4 in 6 chance of hitting for 2 points of damage), but they have also become skilled with spears and curved swords.

Some Black Elves are nomads, travelling the plains in caravans to trade their wares in isolated settlements. Others live in small villages themselves, hunting and farming on the poor land. All Black Elves are distrustful of other beings. They will attack other types of Elves on sight, but other beings will be treated neutrally, if not in a friendly way. They have no love for strangers, and are not averse to waylaying them for their gold.

DARK ELF
SKILL: 8
STAMINA: 6
HABITAT: Dungeons, Ruins, Forests, Plains, Hills
NUMBER ENCOUNTERED: 1–3
TYPE: Humanoid
REACTION: Hostile
INTELLIGENCE: High

In the times before the rise of human civilization, the different Elven races went their separate ways across the world. The taint of evil had split them into two factions. In the wars that followed, the side of Good won, however, and their opponents were forced to retreat beneath the earth, leaving the forests to the Wood Elves. In time all memory of these evil tribes was forgotten. In the darkness of their subterranean world, though, the DARK ELVES grew strong again, and their civilization developed.

Over the centuries their physical form changed, and they became very thin and gaunt, with midnight-black skin and green eyes. Their minds developed too, and they became more and more evil. Their sorcerers began to rule them, and their culture became decadent with slaves, demon worship and grisly magical rituals, for they had perverted the ancient Elven magic to their own ends. They have an inbuilt hatred of all surface-dwellers, and small bands of Dark Elves continue to raid isolated areas, burning and looting whatever they find. When on the surface they shield themselves under large, black, hooded cloaks.

Below ground, however, Dark Elves look very different, dressing in bizarre, ornate clothes and decorating their hair and bodies with strange patterns and colours. Their favourite weapons are still bows, though in the confines below they prefer long serrated knives, fashioned in strange metals and with powerful magic bound into them in jagged ancient runes. Despite their hatred of the surface world, the Dark Elves know they could never return to live there. But their hatred continues unabated, and their raiding parties will always stalk the earth, killing or abducting any they meet.

MOUNTAIN ELF

SKILL: 7
STAMINA: 6
HABITAT: Mountains, Hills, Forests
NUMBER ENCOUNTERED: 1–3
TYPE: Humanoid
REACTION: Neutral
INTELLIGENCE: High

Not all good Elves dwell in the lowland forests. Higher up, on the hills and mountainsides, MOUNTAIN ELVES hunt in the snowy evergreen forests. They look very similar to Wood Elves, though they are shorter and not quite so thin. They dress in warm hides and furs, typically brown or white, and carry bows and long hunting-knives. They are excellent shots, and can hit a target 5 times in 6, for 3 points of STAMINA damage. They live off deer, rabbits and other woodland creatures, though they are careful to take only what they need.

Mountain Elves make their homes in small huts perched high up in trees, which offer protection from the ravages of Snow Wolves and other dangerous predators. Mountain Elves are peaceful, rather shy beings, who do not concern themselves with the affairs of the younger races. They are wary of strangers, but will be helpful if treated with respect. If they are attacked, they will not hesitate to kill their opponents with a deadly volley of arrows.

WOOD ELF

SKILL: 8
STAMINA: 6
HABITAT: Forests
NUMBER ENCOUNTERED: 1–3
TYPE: Humanoid
REACTION: Friendly–Neutral
INTELLIGENCE: High

The most common of all the Elven races are the WOOD ELVES, who may be encountered in any large forest. They are friendly, peaceful beings who love nature and spend much of their time caring for plants, trees and the other denizens of the forests. They don't much care for Dwarfs, because they are unable to understand how they can shut themselves away from the beautiful surface world. Wood Elves loathe Orcs, Trolls and the other inhuman races for their ugliness and their insistence on burning down forests and murdering innocent creatures out of hand. As far as humans are concerned, they are undecided. They know that some are their allies in fighting the forces of Evil, while others are in league with the Orcs and their foul ilk. If adventurers are friendly and respectful, Wood Elves will give them all the help they need. If they prove violent and destructive, they will not be allowed to take another step into the Elves' domain.

Wood Elves prefer to dress in soft green clothes which allow them to blend with their overgrown surroundings. They are skilled in all the woodland crafts, and can track their prey in complete silence until they wish to strike. They are superb bowmen, hitting 5 times in 6 for 3 points of STAMINA damage. In combat they will use shortswords to great effect.

They dwell in large hidden villages protected both by overgrown vegetation and powerful magic. The Wood Elves ensure that only those they trust can find their villages. All others who seek them will become lost and wander around without ever getting near them. In their villages the Elves are ruled over by proud nobles, both great warriors and spell-casters, who rule fairly and justly over all the creatures of the forest.

ELVIN

SKILL: 6
STAMINA: 4
HABITAT: Forests, Hills
NUMBER ENCOUNTERED: 2–7 (1 die plus 1)
TYPE: Humanoid
REACTION: Friendly–Unfriendly
INTELLIGENCE: High

Many people know ELVINS only as strange, twinkling lights that can sometimes be seen dancing among the trees at night, or as snatches of chattering and laughter that will drift down on the wind. Few people ever meet the Elvins of the Shamutanti

Hills face to face; some are totally unaware that they even exist. They are secretive little beings, related to Elves and Woodlings, and dwell in a number of small villages deep in the heart of thick woodland. They are only half a metre tall, with delicate features – slanted eyes, pointed ears, thin limbs. They are immensely mischievous and magical, and seem to spend much of their time playing frivolous pranks on one another, and other unfortunate beings too.

Elvins' magic powers include the ability to fly or hover in the air at will (without wings!). They can also cause a brilliant glow to appear around themselves, so that they can see in the dark. They love to play tricks by suddenly turning off their glow and then tripping up or stealing something from somebody. They expect their victims to take their pranks good-naturedly. If they can't see the joke, the Elvins may decide to teach them a lesson in humour, by attacking them with their shortswords. When flying, an Elvin adds 2 points to its Attack Strength as it dodges about in the air. Once it has been wounded, however, the spell will be broken and it will have to fight on foot. For all their magic, Elvins are fascinated by true sorcery and will be so impressed by a loud or brilliant spell that they may forget their fight and watch with delight.

EYE STINGER

SKILL: 7
STAMINA: 2
HABITAT: Ruins, Dungeons, Wilderness
NUMBER ENCOUNTERED: 1
TYPE: Monster
REACTION: Hostile
INTELLIGENCE: Average

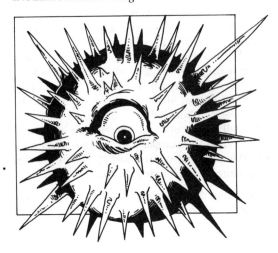

In apparent defiance of all natural laws, the EYE STINGER floats up to a metre above the ground. It is large, spherical and covered with long, poisonous spines. In the centre of its dark green, scaly skin there is a huge staring eye. Anyone encountering an Eye Stinger must successfully *Test for Luck* or be entranced by the eye, and stand slackly as the thing approaches to impale them on its spines. Its poison will not kill them, but just paralyse, leaving the creature or person at the mercy of other creatures. The Eye Stinger will then scavenge any scraps left over.

The hypnotic gaze of an Eye Stinger is very powerful, but it can be disrupted by a pure black object, such as a piece of polished onyx or jet. If it sees such an object, its eye will be confused and will close, allowing its victim to escape.

Anyone striking the creature will be in for a surprise, for the things are mostly full of a sticky liquid which gives off the gas that enables them to 'fly'. When hit, they will burst and splatter everyone fighting them with the acidic liquid, causing 2 points of damage to each person's STAMINA.

FELINAUR

	Adult	Young
SKILL:	9	5
STAMINA:	8	5

HABITAT: Plains
NUMBER ENCOUNTERED: 2–7 (1 die plus 1)
TYPE: Animal/humanoid
REACTION: Neutral
INTELLIGENCE: Average

The FELINAURS of the eastern plains are similar to Centaurs, but whereas the latter are man and horse combined, these creatures are part man and part lion. From the waist upwards, a Felinaur looks much like a normal person, though with a golden-brown, heavily tanned skin and an unkempt mane-like mass of darker brown hair flowing down its back. From the waist downwards, they have the strong, lithe bodies of lions, coloured a sandy golden-brown like their upper halves.

Packs of Felinaurs may be found roaming wide areas of warm grassland, hunting deer and antelope just like their leonine forebears, though using radically more advanced methods! They are expert with bow and javelin, being able to hit a fleeing antelope while galloping along behind it. They also usually carry a shortsword in a scabbard strapped across their backs, next to their quiver. The creatures live in small family groups, clustered together in their own patch of grassland. Both males and females hunt for food, except when the latter have young to rear. Each Felinaur family is part of an extended tribe, ruled over by the strongest male, elected each season after many mock battles and tournaments. It is he who decides which areas to hunt in during the next season, and also has the duty of sacrificing the tribe's first prey of each year to the great Lion God Kurawu, of whom the Felinaurs believe themselves to be the sin-defiled offspring.

Young Felinaurs are very similar to their parents, except that their hindquarters are lightly mottled with spots of darker brown. Felinaurs speak their own language, and also that of lions, with whom they occasionally converse.

FETCH

SKILL: 11
STAMINA: 6
HABITAT: Ruins, Caves, Dungeons
NUMBER ENCOUNTERED: 1–3
TYPE: Magical creature
REACTION: Neutral
INTELLIGENCE: Average

FETCH are strange, magical creatures that are found only rarely, in deserted, out-of-the-way places, particularly around sources of great magic. It is thought they are primitive relatives of Will-o'-the-Wisps, though it has been hard to prove this. A Fetch typically appears as a small, scintillating ball of energy, crackling with static and discharging small bolts of lightning into the air. At the heart of the creature is an intensely glowing area, in which electrical emissions are frequent enough to generate intelligence.

Fetch live off magical energy, and will feed ravenously whenever they can. A Fetch which has not eaten for a week or so will be small and pale; one which has just feasted will be almost a metre across, and very volatile, spitting static in great arcs around itself. A Fetch will attack anyone carrying magical weapons (to suck the items dry), or a particularly heroic adventurer whose aura of luck is tangible enough to feed on! Should they encounter a spell-caster, however, they will deliberately provoke him into casting 'food' at them in the form of spells, by flitting close and attacking in a stinging flash, before nipping away again. Spells flung at a Fetch do it no harm; instead, they will attract more of the creatures, which can scent magical energy from a great distance away.

Fetch are slowed in extreme cold, however, and ice-producing spells will hurt them, and not be eaten. If a metal weapon is used against one in a successful strike, both the wielder and the Fetch will take damage as the creature shorts out! A Dispel Magic spell or charm will destroy one immediately, making it pop out of existence in a small, violent flash.

FIEND

SKILL: 6
STAMINA: 8
HABITAT: Deserts, Ruins
NUMBER ENCOUNTERED: 1–2
TYPE: Monster/humanoid
REACTION: Hostile
INTELLIGENCE: Average

In the heart of the Desert of Skulls all kinds of strange beasts dwell, encountered but rarely by men; the FIEND is one such creature. A remnant from an earlier civilization that colonized the fringes of the desert, it lurks among old ruins, perhaps awaiting the return of its long-dead masters. As tall as man, they are tough, sinewy humanoids, covered in leathery red skin. As well as sharp claws and teeth, they have a pair of horns which sprout from their savage-looking heads. In an attack they will slash about with their claws, and then catch their opponent unawares by breathing a blast of fire straight at him! Hitting on a roll of 1 or 2 on one die, it will cause an additional 1 point of damage. Should it slay its opponent, the Fiend will breathe on it a little more, before feasting on the succulent roasted flesh. Fiends will often be found watching over hoards of priceless ancient artefacts, or perhaps even the tombs of their ancient masters.

FIRE DEMON

SKILL: 10   3 Attacks
STAMINA: 10
HABITAT: Demonic Plane, Caves, Ruins, Dungeons
NUMBER ENCOUNTERED: 1
TYPE: Demon
REACTION: Hostile
INTELLIGENCE: High

There are a whole host of Lesser Demons that dwell in the shadows deep in the Abyss. The most common of these are FIRE DEMONS. They are tall, red-skinned beings, vaguely humanoid in shape, but with large leathery wings, horns, and cloven hoofs for feet. They are violent, impulsive creatures, infamous for absent-mindedly massacring weaker creatures around them in their impatience for action.

Fire Demons are sent to the Earthly Plane as Hell's shock troops, for they are imposing beings who are able to command lesser beings like Orcs with ease. An air of darkness and death hangs around them; weak-willed creatures will flee them immediately. They will usually carry both a whip and a flaming sword, and use first one, then the other, in consecutive attacks. They can also shoot streams of fire from their nostrils. This will hit on a roll of 1–4 on one die, for 2 points of damage. If a Fire Demon is killed, it will be engulfed in its own flames, its spirit released to return home to the Demonic Plane.

FIREFOX

SKILL: 7
STAMINA: 6
HABITAT: Plains, Forests
NUMBER ENCOUNTERED: 1
TYPE: Animal
REACTION: Neutral–Unfriendly
INTELLIGENCE: Average

Foxes are fairly common predators throughout northern Allansia and Kakhabad. Most are content to leave men alone, for they know they are no match for them. To the FIREFOXES of the Forests of Snatta, however, an adventurer is just like a boar or a chicken – food! These beasts are as large as Wolves, covered in a rich fiery-red fur and with a magnificent brush of a tail. They are savage hunters, thinking only of their next meal, which they can sniff out and track with great cunning. Their strength, together with the sharpness of their teeth and claws, is enough to cope with most prey. Should a Firefox find itself losing a fight, it also has other powers to draw upon.

If a Firefox is wounded at any time, in the next round it will suddenly burst into flames and leap on its opponent. If its attack is successful, it will burn them for 5 points of STAMINA damage; if not, the creature will be wounded as usual. This 'flame on' is not without cost to the Firefox, for it will lose 1

SKILL and 1 STAMINA point for the tremendous energy it burns up. After its attack it will return to normal, but every time it is wounded again it will attack in flames the round after, until either the Firefox or its opponent is dead. The fiery-red pelt of a Firefox is very valuable, especially to sorcerers, for it is an essential ingredient in all manner of fire-producing spells and potions.

FIRE SPRITE

SKILL: 7
STAMINA: 4
HABITAT: Magical Plane of Fire, anywhere their
    summoner is
NUMBER ENCOUNTERED: 1–3
TYPE: Magical creature
REACTION: Hostile
INTELLIGENCE: Average

Similar to Devlins, FIRE SPRITES are tiny elemental creatures, normally found on the Plane of Fire. They can be summoned to earth, though, by powerful magic, to fight for their summoner. On this plane they appear to be small, vaguely human-shaped beings, composed entirely of flames. They attack by scorching their opponent; their touch is so hot that it does 3 points of damage instead of the normal 2.

Anything flammable bursts into flames at their touch. Dousing them with water seems actually to make them larger and stronger, feeding the flames rather than extinguishing them. However, smothering them in a heavy cloak or rug will cut off their air, and they will go out, banished back to their home plane in an instant. Fire Sprites are no relation to the tiny earthly Sprites.

FISH MAN

SKILL: 7
STAMINA: 6
HABITAT: Rivers, Lakes, Caves, Marshes
NUMBER ENCOUNTERED: 1
TYPE: Fish/humanoid
REACTION: Unfriendly–Hostile
INTELLIGENCE: Low

Originally the result of some grisly experiments by an evil sorcerer in the Cloudcap Mountains, FISH MEN are strange hybrids between men and fish. They have spindly legs, which support a wide torso. Their heads are fish-like, with huge bulbous eyes and a broad mouth, joining straight on to their bodies without a neck. They are covered completely with small yellow-green scales which drip with water and slime.

The strange creatures have both a fish's gills and a human's lungs, and can thus breathe both air and water. Their scaly nature, however, requires them to keep themselves damp; should they dry out, their skins would crack and they would die. For this reason they will only ever be encountered in or near a large body of water, often a pool inside a shady cave, well away from the sun. Fish Men are solitary beings, full of hatred for the world that shuns them as freaks. However, once a year, at the time of the Spring Equinox, they will gather in an ancient lake in the mountains to spawn, croaking and gurgling at the moon in their husky voices.

Fish Men are not very intelligent, though they have learnt to use spears and javelins stolen from past opponents. They are prodigious meat-eaters, always hungry, and will attack most creatures. They are attracted, almost like magpies, to bright sparkling items, with which they will sometimes decorate the floor of their pool – laying coins, gems and other trinkets in a bizarre underwater mosaic!

FLAYER

SKILL: 6   3 Attacks
STAMINA: 7
HABITAT: Dungeons, Ruins, Towns
NUMBER ENCOUNTERED: 1
TYPE: Humanoid
REACTION: Neutral–Unfriendly
INTELLIGENCE: Average–Low

It is widely believed in educated circles that FLAYERS are somehow related to the ghastly Brain Slayers. Certainly there are many physical similarities between the two races. Flayers have a humanoid body and legs, though they lack arms. Their heads are octopus-like, with a dense fringe of thin prehensile tentacles. Unlike a Brain Slayer, however, their skin is not solid, but is more like grey jelly, which quivers repulsively with every movement. They dress in tatty clothes.

Flayers are rarely seen by men, preferring to secrete themselves away from the attentions of other races. However, it has been discovered that they have somehow developed extraordinary skill at preparing some of the most bizarre, but also the tastiest, dishes. As a result, a Flayer may sometimes be encountered in the unlikely surroundings of a well-equipped kitchen, cooking weird and wonderful meals for the nobleman who can afford to employ it. Their disgusting appearance, though, often causes other creatures and humans to hate and eventually attack them. The reaction they receive from other beings has made the Flayers sad and shy creatures, wary of others and quick to defend themselves. In a fight, a Flayer will whip its head violently from side to side, slashing the air with its tentacles. Each is equipped with a barbed sting that allows it to cause 3 points of damage for a successful hit, instead of the usual 2.

FLESH GRUB

SKILL: 1
STAMINA: 1
HABITAT: Marshes, Dungeons, Ruins, Caves
NUMBER ENCOUNTERED: 2–12
TYPE: Insect
REACTION: Neutral
INTELLIGENCE: None

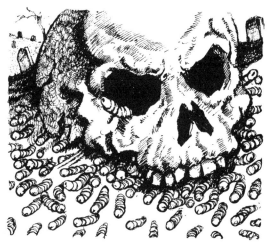

Mooching about in old tombs or dungeons may be the best way for an adventurer to gain fame and fortune, but it is not without its hazards. As well as the larger creatures there are many smaller dangers, such as FLESH GRUBS. These disgusting maggot-like worms lurk writhing in rotting debris and other hidden corners, waiting for the tell-tale scent of human flesh to waft by. They are blind, but can easily smell out their target before latching on to

it with barbed teeth. Each Flesh Grub will automatically inflict 1 point of STAMINA damage as it nibbles away at the fresh meat. The nasty little creatures can be pulled off and crushed easily, but only six can be removed in one round.

GIANT FLY

	Common Fly	Firefly	Needlefly
SKILL:	7	5	6
STAMINA:	8	5	6

HABITAT: Wilderness, Deserts
NUMBER ENCOUNTERED: 1–3
TYPE: Insect
REACTION: Unfriendly
INTELLIGENCE: Low

The various species of GIANT FLY are normally found only in warm regions, where they will be encountered flying around looking for suitable food for themselves and their young. COMMON FLIES can reach one and a half metres in length, with a wingspan twice that. They are disgusting creatures, with huge eyes, black bodies covered with stiff hairs, and a long, sharp proboscis for eating with. They will attack any creature up to and including the size of humans. If it wins an Attack Round, instead of causing damage the Giant Fly will try to fly off with its prey. Unless he can successfully Test for Luck, its victim will be dragged up into the air and dropped, causing 1 die worth of STAMINA damage.

GIANT FIREFLIES are only a third of the size of a Common Fly, but they are just as aggressive. They are only encountered at night, when the rear of their bodies glows in the darkness. If they hit their prey, there is a 3 in 6 chance that they will also deliver a discharge of electricity, causing 2 points of STAMINA damage. NEEDLEFLIES look like enormous hornets, about a metre in length, with a long, sharp sting poking from their tails. They attack with their abdomens curled under them, so that this sting is pointing forwards, and swoop back and forth, trying to stab their prey before carrying it off to eat.

FLYING FISH

SKILL: *8*
STAMINA: *8*
HABITAT: *Lakes*
NUMBER ENCOUNTERED: *2–7 (1 die plus 1)*
TYPE: *Fish*
REACTION: *Unfriendly*
INTELLIGENCE: *Low*

There are FLYING FISH in the warm southern oceans, but none are as dangerous or aggressive as those found in Lake Ilklala in Kakhabad. They are only as long as a man's hand, but their wide mouths brim with teeth which can tear through flesh and bone alike. They can fly for a few minutes at a time, flapping thin, oversized fins like wings. Their long, feathery tails enable them to turn and swoop quite aerobatically, and they can bite while flying. The Flying Fish will attack as a group (treated as a single creature), flapping around their opponent for a maximum of seven Attack Rounds before they must land in the water again. If they land on the ground, they will quickly die, weakly flapping in a vain attempt to reach the lake and safety.

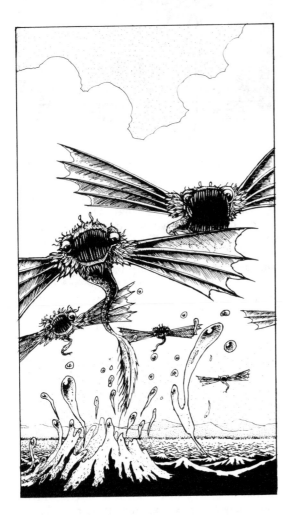

Should anyone be foolish enough to eat one, they will find that its meat tastes foul and causes intense stomach pains for several hours, for one die of STAMINA damage.

FLYING GUARDIAN

SKILL: *8*
STAMINA: *8*
HABITAT: *Ruins, Dungeons*
NUMBER ENCOUNTERED: *2*
TYPE: *Magical creature*
REACTION: *Hostile*
INTELLIGENCE: *Low*

Some very peculiar beings have been left to stand guard over sacred places. In the northern province of Chiang Mai, it is traditional to leave a pair of FLYING GUARDIANS to watch over a tomb or temple. They appear, to all intents and purposes, to be statues in the form of large, ostrich-like birds with hooked beaks, stubby wings and wide, clawed feet. They will remain perfectly rigid, keeping their silent vigil until the treasure or crypt is disturbed by a would-be thief or grave-robber. Then the Guardians will come to life, take to the air with strangely stilted, jerky movements, and attack with beaks and claws. They may also try to warn other denizens of the tomb, if there are any, by croaking loudly like a crow. When they have dealt with the defilers of their sacred home, they will return to their positions and stiffen into statues to continue their silent watch.

FOG DEVIL

SKILL: *8*
STAMINA: *6*
HABITAT: *Forests*
NUMBER ENCOUNTERED: *1–3*
TYPE: *Monster*
REACTION: *Unfriendly–Hostile*
INTELLIGENCE: *Low*

When the mists of winter descend on the tangled hearts of forests, the FOG DEVILS gather amid the trees to hunt and play. Streaming through the trees, howling and screaming like demented Wolves, they roam in search of Woodlings or Gnomes to feast upon.

These strange and savage monsters appear as ghostly, billowing concentrations of vapour formed into vaguely human shapes. Their heads have the most definition; from here their bodies gradually trail away into nothingness and merge with the mist. Their faces are misshapen, nightmarish parodies of a human visage, with insane eyes and a fang-filled slash of a mouth. Their arms appear to be strong and muscular, ending in three-fingered hands which can rend a man in two with a single slash. In an attack, a swirling Fog Devil will spin around an opponent in a confusing spiral of mist that suddenly sprouts claws and teeth. Anyone attacked by such a creature will fight it with their SKILL reduced by 2 for the duration of the encounter. Should the creatures kill their opponent, they will stop briefly to nibble on the choicest parts, before swirling on.

Thankfully for the other denizens of the forests, these savage, evil beings are very rare, and will only be encountered when the thickest winter fogs are in the air. For the rest of the time, the Fog Devils hibernate in the boles of trees and forgotten animal burrows, waiting for the mists to come again.

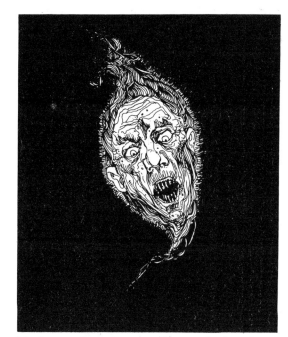

Most are souls passing up or down to the domains of their respective Deities. Some beings dwell permanently on the Spirit Plane itself: Poltergeists are trapped here because of the nature of their deaths. But the GANJEES live here on purpose.

Related to Ghosts but far more hateful, these non-corporeal entities are little more than a small concentration of energy, driven by spite and anger, but they can appear to their victims as ghostly white faces, contorted with devilish glee. Anyone who meets one for the first time must immediately lose 1 SKILL and 2 STAMINA points from sheer terror! Ganjees can extinguish flames, throw objects and even wield weapons. Fighting back against them, though, is very difficult, because they do not have physical bodies. However, they can sometimes be bribed to let someone pass freely, by the gift of a magical item such as a potion or sword – though they are just as likely to forget all about their bargain and use these very items against the adventurer!

GANJEE

SKILL: 12
STAMINA: 0 (see below)
HABITAT: Ruins, Dungeons, Caves
NUMBER ENCOUNTERED: 1–6
TYPE: Undead
REACTION: Hostile
INTELLIGENCE: High

Between the Earthly Plane and the Magical Planes is a nebulous layer known as the Spirit Plane. Its inhabitants dwell half in the world and half out of it.

GARGOYLE

SKILL: 9   2 Attacks
STAMINA: 10
HABITAT: Caves, Ruins, Dungeons
NUMBER ENCOUNTERED: 1–2
TYPE: Monster
REACTION: Hostile
INTELLIGENCE: Average–Low

GARGOYLES are ferocious beasts, whose ability to blend with the surrounding rock is such that they will surprise a prey 5 times out of 6, and be able to deliver their first blow automatically. They are roughly humanoid in shape, with clawed hands and feet, and bestial heads brimming with teeth and horns. A pair of large leathery wings sprouts from their backs, and a point-tipped tail hangs behind. They are coloured a mottled grey that looks just like stone. This camouflage allows them to play their favourite trick on an adventurer – standing motionless on a piece of stone and pretending to be a statue until they can strike.

The stony hide of a Gargoyle is tough: normal weapons cannot injure them. In fact, two blows on a Gargoyle are enough to break even the strongest of swords. Enchanted magical weapons can injure them, however, and they will also retreat from fire. It is rumoured that the Gargoyles pay fealty, in both service and treasure, to the evil Night Demon Vradna, who is said to be served by a legion of a thousand of the foul creatures.

GARK

SKILL: 7
STAMINA: 11
HABITAT: Plains, Forests, Hills, Ruins, Caves,
    Dungeons
NUMBER ENCOUNTERED: 1
TYPE: Humanoid
REACTION: Unfriendly
INTELLIGENCE: Low

In the huge vats of dungeon-like laboratories deep below the surface of the earth, evil sorcerers have long experimented with cross-breeding the various inhuman races – Orcs, Goblins, Ogres, Trolls and Giants. Combining Orc and Troll they have produced the warlike Doragar; mixing Goblin and Giant they created the GARK.

They look very much like a huge Goblin, well over two and a half metres tall. They are lithe, muscular and very aggressive. Their brown hides are tough and leathery, and they can prove to be formidable warriors with axes and cleavers. They are not overly intelligent, however, and can sometimes be very unpredictable, especially in the heat of battle. In the colonies of Goblins and Orcs in which they dwell, they will usually be found on guard-duty in some forgotten corner where they cannot damage anything. Garks are attracted to pretty, sparkling things, and they may possess whole trunks full of worthless trinkets that have caught their eye.

GENIE

SKILL: 12
STAMINA: 20
HABITAT: Magical Planes, anywhere their summoner
    is
NUMBER ENCOUNTERED: 1
TYPE: Magical creature
REACTION: Neutral
INTELLIGENCE: High

GENIES are magical creatures who can pop up in the most unlikely places to help or hinder a frustrated adventurer. They seem very Chaotic beings, but in truth they serve the Trickster Gods of Luck and Chance. These mysterious Deities delight in manipulating the aims of both Good and Evil for their own amusement. If Evil looks as though it is winning at something, they will try to influence events so that Good starts to gain the upper hand, and vice versa.

To affect events like this they use the Genies. These beings usually dwell on the Magical Planes in spirit form. When they are sent to the Earthly Plane they will assume a more substantial shape, typically that of a wispy humanoid, fat and bald, who will float in the air as if levitating. The help a Genie offers can be most infuriating at times, but at others it can be very helpful. They may divert enemies, turn an adventurer invisible, or even offer him a free wish! Such aid is rarely completely to the benefit of the adventurer; wishes, especially, tend to be twisted and taken so literally that they are more trouble to their user than they are worth. Such behaviour makes some people dislike Genies intensely. Anyone trying to attack a Genie will be in for a shock, though, for weapons will pass straight through their bodies without harming them. In return, a Genie might decide to teach such an ungrateful person a lesson that will ensure he is more polite to the servants of Fate in the future!

immobile and ready to be devoured. If a Ghoul manages to hit someone four times, he will be unable to move or speak, or indeed do anything else at all. His whole body will go numb, his breathing will become more and more constricted, and he can only wait to be eaten.

GIANT

GHOUL

SKILL: 8   2 Attacks
STAMINA: 7
HABITAT: Ruins, Dungeons
NUMBER ENCOUNTERED: 1–3
TYPE: Undead
REACTION: Hostile
INTELLIGENCE: Low

Once, perhaps, they were human, but not now. GHOULS are noxious undead creatures whose spirits hover halfway between life and death. They dwell in tombs and crypts, for they eat corpses – especially those of humans. They look very much as though they are dead themselves, with rotting, maggot-ridden skin only half hiding their decaying innards. Their tongues loll from sickly, grinning mouths as they hiss with delight at the prospect of fresh meat. They will attack with their clawed hands, slashing violently about them, apparently unafraid of the swords held against them. The hands of a Ghoul carry further dangers, for they have the power to paralyse their prey, leaving him

GIANTS are basically large humanoids, growing up to five times the height of the average human. There are a number of different species of Giant, scattered widely across different parts of the world. They are, on the whole, blustery, quick-tempered beings, often forgetful of their great size. They stomp about the world, crushing trees and dwellings in their path without a thought. At other times, however, they will pay great attention to the 'little people'. They may 'play' with them – lifting them up and dropping them again, taking the roofs off their houses to peer curiously inside, and so on. But when they feel hungry, they may gather them up and eat them as snacks.

Because of their Chaotic natures, Giants are greatly feared by many inhabitants of wilder regions. Thankfully, most Giants are rather dim; if they were ever organized into a disciplined army they could tear down whole cities. The various different races often fight among themselves, which keeps their attention away from smaller beings for most of the time.

CAVE GIANT

SKILL: 9   2 Attacks
STAMINA: 10
HABITAT: Caves, Dungeons
NUMBER ENCOUNTERED: 1–3
TYPE: Humanoid
REACTION: Hostile
INTELLIGENCE: Low

CAVE GIANTS are the smallest of all Giants, growing to little more than three metres tall – and appearing to be even shorter, because their backs are hunched over from life in their low-ceilinged tunnels. They only dwell underground, living on other denizens of the darkness. Their skins are light grey in colour and hairless, enabling them to blend with their surroundings and surprise their prey (for one automatic blow) 5 times in 6. Their silvery eyes have grown dim from peering in the subterranean gloom, and they will be blinded by the sudden appearance of bright light. A Cave Giant will be wearing a loincloth and carrying a stone club or a sack of throwing-rocks. They are unintelligent beings, and will attack almost everything. They especially love the tender flesh of Troglodytes,

which they scoop up to chew on when they are hungry.

FOREST GIANT

SKILL: 9   2 Attacks
STAMINA: 9
HABITAT: Forests
NUMBER ENCOUNTERED: 1
TYPE: Humanoid
REACTION: Unfriendly
INTELLIGENCE: Average

Fully grown FOREST GIANTS can be as much as five metres tall. They are muscular beings, typically dressed in rough brown or green clothes of fur and cloth, with ruddy-brown skin and unkempt hair. They will be carrying a huge club made from the large branch of a tree, or a stone-headed axe, and sometimes a sack containing a few Gold Pieces, some food, and maybe even a few choice rocks for throwing.

Unlike many Giants, this race cares for its habitat, and tends the trees of the forest. They are sometimes friendly with Tree Men and Wood Elves, though they often come into conflict with the former. While Forest Giants may tend young trees and bushes, they have no qualms about chopping down larger ones for firewood! Like the other races, though, they don't take kindly to trespassers in their domains and will attempt to remove them. They will throw rocks from a distance (hitting on a roll of 1–4 on one die, for 3 points of damage), before closing to finish them off with their clubs. They are not averse to eating humans, though they find them a little stringy and unsatisfying; they prefer deer or boar.

FROST GIANT

SKILL: 10   3 Attacks
STAMINA: 10
HABITAT: Ice, Wilderness, Caves, Mountains
NUMBER ENCOUNTERED: 1
TYPE: Humanoid
REACTION: Hostile
INTELLIGENCE: Average

FROST GIANTS, which can grow up to six metres tall, live only in the coldest regions, such as the ice plains north of the craggy Icefinger Mountains.

Their skin is pale white, but much of it is usually hidden by their long white beards and hair, and under swathes of Polar Bear fur. They are solitary beings, preferring the company of Snow Wolves to that of other Frost Giants. If encountered out hunting, a Frost Giant will be accompanied by 1–6 Snow Wolves. They live on the meat of any creature they can catch. They will stay clear of Toa-Suo, however, for they fear that they will be overwhelmed by sheer force of numbers. Frost Giants are not afraid of attacking humans, for they know that the little beings may also be carrying Gold, which Frost Giants dearly love to hoard in their caves.

HILL GIANT

SKILL: 9   2 Attacks
STAMINA: 11
HABITAT: Hills, Caves
NUMBER ENCOUNTERED: 1–2
TYPE: Humanoid
REACTION: Hostile
INTELLIGENCE: Average

HILL GIANTS are lumpy, ugly brutes that grow up to seven metres tall. They are also fat, hairy and quite repulsive; they are usually dressed in tatty furs and skins. Their favourite weapons are huge wooden clubs, but they also enjoy throwing large rocks down on smaller creatures or on villages. Each rock will hit its target 3 times out of 6, causing 1 die of STAMINA damage to its target. These beings make their homes in large caves, which they sometimes share with Bears and which the latter help to guard. For this the creatures are rewarded with a regular supply of food. The favourite provender of Hill Giants is human flesh, and their caves may have a corner reserved for a 'larder', with many cured joints hanging waiting to be eaten.

MARSH GIANT

SKILL: 9   2 Attacks
STAMINA: 9
HABITAT: Marshes
NUMBER ENCOUNTERED: 1–3
TYPE: Humanoid
REACTION: Hostile
INTELLIGENCE: Average

Green-skinned and scaly, MARSH GIANTS are very different to most other Giants. About six metres tall, they are thin, with membranes between their arms and sides, and wide webbed feet to help them swim. They dwell deep in swamps and marshes, and spend most of their time submerged in the slime hunting for food. They live mostly off small humanoids like Marsh Hoppers and Koko-mokoa, but they may also attack humans who venture into their domain. They will overturn rafts and hold their victims underwater until they drown, before dragging them out again and eating them.

MOUNTAIN GIANT

SKILL: 10   3 Attacks
STAMINA: 12
HABITAT: Mountains, Caves, Ice
NUMBER ENCOUNTERED: 1
TYPE: Humanoid
REACTION: Hostile
INTELLIGENCE: Average

MOUNTAIN GIANTS are only found among the highest peaks of large ranges. They can reach as much as eight metres in height; their bodies are hefty and muscular. They are usually clad in thick furs and hides, and will be carrying large stone clubs or axes. Mountain Giants are very strong and can uproot trees and huge boulders to throw at their opponents. These have a 3 in 6 chance of hitting, for one die plus one point of damage.

A Mountain Giant may keep a Giant Eagle as a pet or for hunting, training it to attack intruders into his or her domain. They are solitary beings and are very avaricious, hoarding gold and other treasure in their caverns high in the clouds. When encountered away from their lairs, they will usually be carrying a large sack holding a few Gold Pieces, several throwing-rocks and a few scraps of food (a couple of boars, half a cow, or some other light snack).

SEA GIANT

SKILL: 10   3 Attacks
STAMINA: 17
HABITAT: Sea
NUMBER ENCOUNTERED: 1
TYPE: Humanoid
REACTION: Unfriendly
INTELLIGENCE: Average

The largest of all Giants dwell not on the land, but

underwater. SEA GIANTS are enormous blue-skinned beings that can reach ten metres tall. Their feet and hands are webbed, and their hair flows in tresses over their scaly bodies. They are said by superstitious sailors to be responsible for storms and whirlpools at sea. Certainly they dislike the intrusion of large vessels into their domains, and may make their presence known. Common tactics include sending great waves to swamp boats, or rearing out of the water to overturn them.

Sea Giants can breathe both air and water, but never venture on land. When swimming in the open ocean they may be accompanied by Dolphins or Merfolk, with whom they are friendly. They make their lairs in great caves on the sea-bed, which they decorate with treasure taken from sunken ships, by plastering the walls with coins and littering the floor with jewels.

STORM GIANT
SKILL: 10   4 Attacks
STAMINA: 15
HABITAT: Mountains, Wilderness
NUMBER ENCOUNTERED: 1
TYPE: Humanoid
REACTION: Neutral–Unfriendly
INTELLIGENCE: High

In vast stone castles perched above the clouds, on top of the jagged peaks of high mountains, solitary STORM GIANTS look down on the world of Giants and men alike with disdain. They are great scholars, their hawks gathering news from the farthest lands for them. Unlike other Giants, they are very intelligent, and have been the keepers of the wisdom of ancient times for many centuries. In their secluded castles are stored books, scrolls, devices and machines from past ages, most of which are unintelligible to a modern sorcerer or sage.

A Storm Giant is typically eight metres tall, thin but muscular, with pale skin and yellow hair. They dress in fine robes and may be carrying a huge staff. From their lofty peaks they sometimes dabble in the affairs of others by changing the weather. They can send rain, heatwaves and even violent electrical storms down from their castles to influence the actions of armies or fleets. More often, however, they will use their powers to help the land itself in times of flood or drought.

Their castles may be shared with Giant Eagles or Air Elementals, with whom they are friendly. They will be spartan, devoid of decoration and with plain furniture and fittings. Their libraries and observatories are more opulent, and crammed with relics.

GNOME

SKILL: 7
STAMINA: 5
HABITAT: Forests, Hills, Caves, Dungeons
NUMBER ENCOUNTERED: 1
TYPE: Humanoid
REACTION: Unfriendly
INTELLIGENCE: High

Grumpy, crotchety beings, GNOMES shun the affairs of other creatures. They are small humanoids, related distantly to Dwarfs, and may be encountered in remote areas. They prefer to be left alone, free from the attentions of other races, who seem only to bring violence and other complications to their simple lives. They will prove most unfriendly if disturbed by a rude human, sometimes suddenly attacking with their small axes, sometimes using magic. Gnomes can perform all kinds of subtle magic, but will use it mostly to defend themselves, by turning invisible, making a sword go limp in its wielder's hands and so on. A Gnome will not normally use its magic to attack someone who unwittingly disturbs it, but if he continues to do so, he may find himself on the wrong end of a lightning bolt, or some other clear warning to leave the Gnome alone!

GOBLIN

	Goblin	Marsh Goblin
SKILL:	5	6
STAMINA:	5	6

HABITAT: Hills, Plains, Wilderness, Caves, Dungeons, Marshes
NUMBER ENCOUNTERED: 1–6
TYPE: Humanoid
REACTION: Hostile
INTELLIGENCE: Average

GOLEMS are magical humanoids animated by sorcerers to serve them. Similar to Crystal Warriors, but far more flexible in their uses, they make excellent guards or servants, for they are strong, unsleeping and totally obedient. The creation of a Golem requires powerful magic and a day-long ritual. Some spell-casters have managed, however, to devise a spell that allows them to create a Golem instantly from a large mass of the appropriate material. By pointing a finger at a chair, for example, and muttering a few lines, a sorcerer can transform the object into a large wooden humanoid that will do his every wish.

FLESH GOLEMS are animated from the dead bodies of humans, typically sewn together to create an ugly, disjointed figure almost three metres tall. Like all Golems, they are deaf to all but the voice of their master or mistress, and cannot speak. They attack with club-like fists, smashing their way through armour and bones alike.

Smaller than Orcs but just as disgusting, GOBLINS are crude humanoids that are found causing trouble in many lands. They are ugly, brown-skinned beings, about a metre and a half tall, typically dressed in ragged furs, hides and scraps of armour. Goblins are evil creatures who delight in enslaving, torturing and killing humans, Dwarfs and Elves. Some still dwell in primitive villages in the wilderness, but most now serve alongside Orcs, Ogres and Trolls in the inhuman armies of Chaos. Like most of their cousins they prefer to live underground, away from sunlight which annoys them with its brightness.

Goblins are typically armed with swords, small axes or throwing-daggers (these hit on a roll of 1–3 on one die, for 3 STAMINA points of damage). They also like making cruel traps for unwary creatures to stumble into. These can include deep pits full of poison-tipped spikes, barbed man-traps and a number of other nasty devices. Each tribe of Goblins will be led by a stronger warrior (SKILL 7, STAMINA 6), at the front of any attack.

MARSH GOBLINS are similar to common Goblins, but with a few notable differences. They are thinner, with green-tinted, almost scaly skins, and their hands and feet are webbed for swimming. They spend most of their time skulking in the mud and reeds of their swampland homes, often raiding Kokomokoa, whom they hate. Marsh Goblins like humans even less than their land-based relatives do, and they delight, for example, in tying a captive to a board and leaving him for Giant Leeches to drain slowly of blood . . .

GOLEM

	Flesh Golem	Stone Golem	Wood Golem	
SKILL:	8	8	8	2 Attacks
STAMINA:	7	11	6	

HABITAT: Anywhere their master is
NUMBER ENCOUNTERED: 1
TYPE: Magical creature
REACTION: Hostile
INTELLIGENCE: Low

The strongest of the three types are STONE GOLEMS, large powerful beings that are easily mistaken for statues when stationary. They are created from a single block of stone, which is normally carved to the desired shape before being animated. Stone Golems are sometimes deliberately made exactly like statues, so that they can discreetly guard certain areas and catch intruders unawares. Others are made to look more human and will usually be more active in the service of their masters. They will attack with their large stone hands; if they have been posing as a statue, they may also be carrying a stone weapon. Their bodies are so hard that edged weapons – swords, axes, spears and arrows – have no effect on them at all. A crushing weapon such as a mace or war-hammer will do normal damage to a Stone Golem.

WOOD GOLEMS do not have to be carved from one

single log, but all the wood must be from the same tree. Wood Golems, once animated, are completely invulnerable to magic of all kinds; even a magical weapon will be no better than an ordinary one. They are very vulnerable to fire, however, which can turn them into a blazing torch in a few short moments. Wood Golems attack with their hands, causing normal damage.

If the Gonchong misses, it will fall to the floor, and while it readies itself for another attempt it can be dispatched easily. Should the thing hit its target, however, its proboscis will puncture the new host's head while it grips with its legs. The victim will become a soulless host for the evil Gonchong – strong beyond belief, but condemned to a deathly existence as its slave.

GONCHONG

SKILL: 5
STAMINA: 5
HABITAT: Anywhere their victim is
NUMBER ENCOUNTERED: 1
TYPE: Monster
REACTION: Hostile
INTELLIGENCE: High

If there was ever a creature that should not live, it is the GONCHONG. It is a cruel, evil parasite which takes control of the brain of its victim and uses it to commit horrendous atrocities. It looks rather like a huge bony spider or crab, with a pair of small, staring eyes on stalks at the front of its body. It is physically weak, and uses its evil intelligence instead to achieve its gruesome ends.

The thing will choose a powerful leader – a king, general or high sorcerer – and latch on to his head by skewering a long proboscis through the top and into the brain. This thin tube must be severed to kill the Gonchong. However, the creature instils great physical powers in its host (adding 5 points to both SKILL and STAMINA), so that as the host is defending himself, he is defending the parasitic Gonchong too. The host of a Gonchong cannot be harmed by normal weapons: only an enchanted fire-sword will break the parasite's defences and injure its host. As soon as the host has been killed, the linking proboscis must be severed while it is still stuck in the dead creature's head. Otherwise, the foul thing will withdraw and attempt to leap on to a new victim. Avoiding such a move requires the target to roll his SKILL or less on two dice.

GRANNIT

SKILL: 4
STAMINA: 3
HABITAT: Caves, Dungeons
NUMBER ENCOUNTERED: 1–6
TYPE: Monster
REACTION: Unfriendly–Hostile
INTELLIGENCE: Low

Scuttling around their darkened caves in search of tasty morsels, GRANNITS are surprisingly ferocious little horrors. About the size of a coconut, they are covered in armadillo-like bony armour that blends well with their surroundings and makes stationary Grannits indistinguishable from the rocks and stones around them. This camouflage allows them to surprise their prey as they suddenly scurry on eight tiny legs and sink their teeth into exposed flesh. This first attack inevitably causes 1 point of STAMINA damage to their prey; after this they can be fought normally.

GREMLIN

	Wingless Gremlin	Winged Gremlin
SKILL:	4	5
STAMINA:	3	4

HABITAT: Caves, Ruins, Forests, Dungeons
NUMBER ENCOUNTERED: 1–3
TYPE: Humanoid
REACTION: Hostile
INTELLIGENCE: Average–High

GREMLINS are tiny humanoids found lurking in underground caverns where they live off small insects and animals. WINGLESS GREMLINS stand up to half a metre tall, though they are often much shorter than this. They have thin bodies supporting large heads, greenish skins, long noses and pointed ears. They dress in ragged clothes of sackcloth or animal hide, and carry short daggers. They are nasty little creatures, who will not hesitate to attack beings much larger than themselves. They are skilled at burrowing through the earth, and may infest a dungeon complex with a myriad tiny tunnels between the larger passages.

Their cousins, WINGED GREMLINS, are smaller and thinner, but just as evil. They grow only to about fifteen centimetres tall, with tiny leathery wings sprouting from their backs, but in all other respects they are similar to their larger, wingless relations. They make ideal familiars for wizards, and are often sent by them to gather ingredients or spy on enemies. They are too small to use weapons effectively, but they can bite with their sharp little teeth.

GRETCH

SKILL: 10
STAMINA: 13
HABITAT: Deserts
NUMBER ENCOUNTERED: 1–3
TYPE: Monster
REACTION: Hostile
INTELLIGENCE: Low

Not even the wisest desert nomads can tell where a GRETCH is hidden deep under the sands, waiting to surprise its unwary prey. The creatures are highly skilled at covering their tracks, and then burying themselves under the sand without a trace, leaving only two minute holes for their keen eyes to watch for the approach of a suitable meal. Gretch are thin, sandy-coloured reptilian monsters, which usually walk on their hind legs, standing as tall as a man. They have large heads, like that of a snake or lizard, with forked tongues and wide fang-filled mouths. Each scaly hand ends in one long claw, like a cruel curved dagger, honed and sharpened until it can slice through skin and bone alike.

Gretch are cold-blooded creatures, and can survive well in the baking heat of the desert, though even they must shelter from its might as midday approaches, under the cooling sands. They are carnivorous, and will hide near water-holes and popular caravan routes, to prey on travellers and their mounts. They bury themselves and wait. When a suitable meal approaches, they will burst out of the sand and pounce on their surprised prey. Their claws are so sharp that they will do 3 points of damage in a successful hit. Their constant need for food makes them fight to the death, for an injured Gretch will die a slow, painful death from starvation, unable to capture its much-needed food.

HAMAKEI

SKILL: 7
STAMINA: 5
HABITAT: Deserts, Ruins
NUMBER ENCOUNTERED: 1
TYPE: Humanoid
REACTION: Neutral
INTELLIGENCE: High

Perched in towers hidden in the desert wastelands, the HAMAKEI are the last remnants of a past, more sorcerous age. Centuries old, these brittle, withered humanoids have vulture-like heads, and are usually swathed in masses of fine robes. They are warlocks and sages, kept alive well beyond their normal span by arcane spells and magical artefacts. Their powers are wide, gleaned from decades of research in forgotten libraries, but they use them only rarely. The Hamakei see themselves as scholars and observers, and will rarely be drawn into the petty conflicts of mortal men. Their lust is only for knowledge, and their advice can sometimes be traded for an old scroll or ancient device.

As crotchety as an ancient owl, they can be extremely temperamental and absent-minded, but will swiftly turn from doddering fool to wily fox at the mention of lost knowledge. Occasionally a Hamakei will set out into the world of men, wandering from settlement to settlement in search of any snippet it can overhear. Some are interested in the progress of this younger age and will seek out human sorcerers, to see how much of the lost arts they have rediscovered.

If encountered away from its home, a Hamakei will be dressed in inconspicuous travelling-clothes, and will lean on a long staff to help it along. The staff will usualy be magical and may have spells bound into it. In the event of a direct attack, a Hamakei can call upon many spells to ward off attackers, including magical dusts that blind or charm an opponent, and jets and walls of flame and ice. If such attacks fail to repel an aggressor, it will be forced to use its staff to defend itself as best it can.

Their towers will usually be defended by a host of magical traps, to keep intruders away. Their treasure-hoard will be large, consisting for the most part of hundreds of unintelligible and very, very ancient books, scrolls and papers, with a few strange artefacts scattered among them. Any sage worth his salt would pay dearly for even a glimpse of such treasures, though they may appear all but worthless to an adventurer.

HARPY

SKILL: 7
STAMINA: 6
HABITAT: Wilderness, Hills, Mountains
NUMBER ENCOUNTERED: 1–3
TYPE: Monster
REACTION: Hostile
INTELLIGENCE: Low

Legends have long talked of the HARPIES, foul winged creatures that terrorize travellers in desolate lands. They are roughly humanoid with ugly, over-large heads and thin stunted bodies. Stretched between their limbs are vast leathery wings which make them look like human bats! Their feet are bird-like and end in large pointed claws. The vile things delight in tormenting lone travellers and adventurers, swooping down from the sky, cawing and screeching, to buffet them with their wings and slash them with their claws. They appear to have an almost limitless capacity for tormenting their victims, but eventually they will tire of their game and finish them off, before dividing up the bodies and flying off to eat in their lairs (usually a cave or ledge high up a cliff from where they can see a potential plaything kilometres away).

Doragar Christos Achilleos
Night Demon Julek Heller
Brain Slayer Terry Oakes
Fog Devil Alan Craddock
Life-Stealer Ian Miller
Dracon Julek Heller
Dark Elf Mark Bromley
Shapechanger Iain McCaig

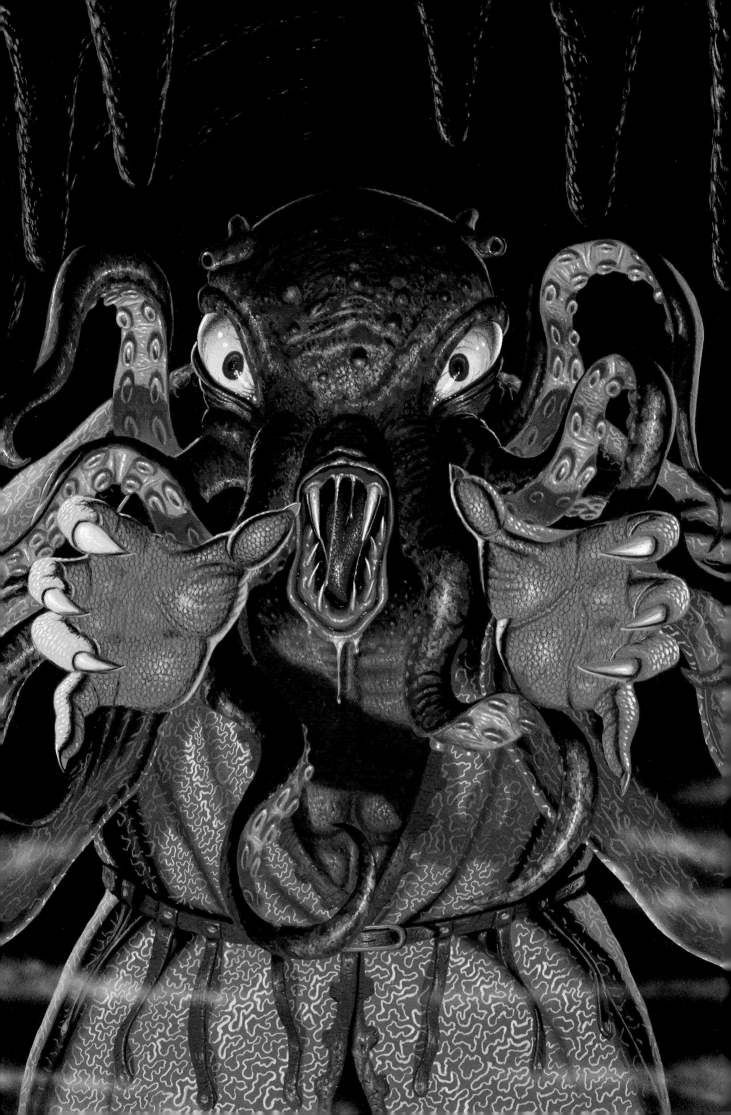

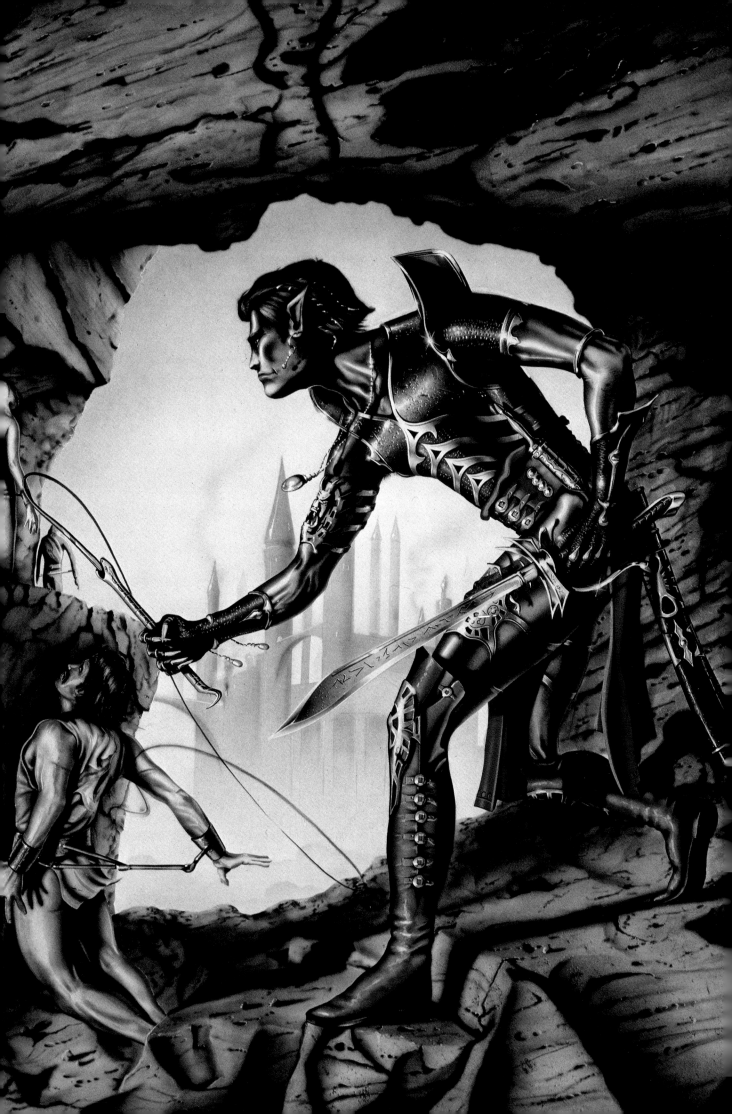

HARRUN

SKILL: 6
STAMINA: 7
HABITAT: Jungles, Mountains
NUMBER ENCOUNTERED: 1–3
TYPE: Animal
REACTION: Neutral
INTELLIGENCE: Low

In the remote jungles of the east, apes have evolved and adapted to their environment in many ways. In the tree canopy many metres above the ground, the six-armed Krell swing on the hanging vines and lianas with incredible dexterity. Similarly, where the jungle meets the mountains, the HARRUN have arisen, and evolved to suit their environment.

These creatures look like small apes, except for the thin, membrane-like wings which stretch from wrists to hips. They have long, flattened tails which help them maintain their balance during their short flights. A Harrun typically launches itself from the top of a high tree, and can swoop for up to half a kilometre down the hillside, with arms spread wide and legs drawn up. Harrun live on fruit and small creatures, but are particularly fond of squirrels and the like, which they will chase across the tree-tops in death-defying leaps and glides.

Harrun live in small family groups in the trees, and in fact spend most of their lives above the ground. They are very inquisitive creatures, and will soar down, chattering excitedly, to investigate any strangers in the forest. This may frighten a nervous adventurer into thinking he is being attacked by the creatures. Despite this, Harrun have never been known to attack anything larger than themselves, except in defence.

HAWK

	Death Hawk	Night Hawk
SKILL:	4	7
STAMINA:	5	5

HABITAT: Hills, Plains, Wilderness
NUMBER ENCOUNTERED: 1–3
TYPE: Bird
REACTION: Neutral–Hostile
INTELLIGENCE: Average–Low

There are times when a message must be sent more quickly than a horse can rides or into a normally inaccessible area. For these reasons many people keep HAWKS, especially trained to carry messages tied to their legs and to fight off any attackers.

DEATH HAWKS, so called because in primitive times they were thought to be the message-carriers of the Gods themselves, are jet-black in colour with reddened eyes and large talons. With a wingspan approaching a metre across, they are not small birds, though they are sometimes mistaken for crows or ravens when seen from a distance. They are not very clever, about as smart as homing-pigeons, but they are plucky fighters.

The large NIGHT HAWKS are more clever, and are able to fly and attack in formation. When a line of the large black birds begins to dive out of the sky, one after the other in perfect order, only the bravest of opponents will stand his ground! These creatures are the favourite pets of a number of evil men, for they make superb guards, since they are able to patrol a wide area of land much more easily than a foot patrol, and with their keen eyes pick out intruders from as much as a kilometre away before swooping down to attack.

HEAD-HUNTER

SKILL: 7
STAMINA: 6
HABITAT: Jungles, Forests
NUMBER ENCOUNTERED: 1–6
TYPE: Humanoid
REACTION: Hostile
INTELLIGENCE: Average

In the depths of the jungle live small tribes of brutish primitives. They are known as HEAD-HUNTERS because of their grisly habit of boiling and curing the heads of their victims until they have shrunk down to a quarter of their normal size. These are then worn as decoration, tied to their loincloths to indicate their prowess as warriors. They are cannibals, preying on other tribes, especially the weaker Pygmies, whenever they need food.

They dress only in loincloths and war-paint, with feathers tied in their hair. Their favourite weapons are clubs and spears, which they tip with carved flint. Head-hunters dwell in small villages, in which three to eighteen (three dice) of them will be encountered. Each tribe is ruled over by a powerful medicine man, a direct link between the superstitious primitives and their many vengeful Gods. The shaman will be wearing a ceremonial mask and many pieces of crude jewellery to indicate his status among the rest of the tribe.

HELL DEMON

SKILL: 14   4 Attacks
STAMINA: 12
HABITAT: Demonic Plane, Ruins, Dungeons
NUMBER ENCOUNTERED: 1
TYPE: Demon
REACTION: Hostile
INTELLIGENCE: Average–High

Spawned from the eternal fires that forever rage in the depths of the Abyss, HELL DEMONS are among the strongest of the Lesser Demons. They are highly trusted by the Demon Princes, and are sent on many missions to the Earthly Plane. They are able to assume the form of any human they encounter, usually killing and eating the person after they have copied him. This allows them to move secretly among men, instilling evil into the heart of civilization.

In their 'normal' form, they are truly horrific beasts. Three metres high, covered in scaly black skin, they hiss steam and sulphurous vapours from their fanged mouths. Their heads are large and misshapen, with long horns curving from the top. Their bodies are muscular, their hands tipped with hooked claws. Their legs end in cloven, goat-like hoofs; a long rat's tail lashes behind them. As if all this wasn't enough to drive a rational man insane, they have a further facet. Their origins in the Abyss have left them immune to blows from normal weapons; only those forged in the eternal fires themselves can pierce their skin.

Some initiates, members of evil Demon-worshipping cults, may carry wavy-bladed kris knives tempered in such flames for use in rituals and sacrifices. Such weapons are exceedingly rare, but it is very advisable to be carrying one when you come face to ghastly face with a raging Hell Demon!

HELLHOUND

SKILL: 7   2 Attacks
STAMINA: 6
HABITAT: Demonic Plane, Dungeons, Ruins
NUMBER ENCOUNTERED: 1–2
TYPE: Monster
REACTION: Hostile
INTELLIGENCE: Low

Many Demon Princes like to keep pets. Sith, a noxious Snake Demon, has a python twenty metres long and a metre thick. Some of the more sophisticated Princes, however, keep a pack of HELL-HOUNDS. The huge dogs are bad-tempered and violent, and therefore make wonderful pets for the vile Demon Princes, who use them in the Wild Hunt, when all the Princes of Hell chase across the Earthly Plane in search of errant human souls.

The beasts are huge, midnight-black dogs, about the size of a Wolf, with black teeth and tongues, and brilliant red eyes. Their bite would be savage enough, but they can also shoot bursts of fire from their mouths. As well as their usual attack, each round the flames will singe their opponent on a roll of 1 or 2 (on one die) for a further 1 point of damage. They can even claw at one opponent and breathe gouts of flame at another.

Hellhounds are usually confined to the Demonic Plane. Some evil sorcerers have managed to summon them to the Earthly Plane, but the beasts are usually too savage to be kept as anything except guard-dogs, roaming empty rooms for intruders to stumble upon.

chieftains or any form of organized society; they just gather together for mutual protection from the ravages of larger creatures and other more warlike tribes.

WILD HILL MAN

SKILL: 6
STAMINA: 5
HABITAT: Hills, Forests, Caves
NUMBER ENCOUNTERED: 1–3
TYPE: Humanoid
REACTION: Unfriendly–Hostile
INTELLIGENCE: Average

The WILD HILL MEN of the Moonstone Hills in eastern Allansia are a race of primitive humans related to Cavemen and Neanderthals, though they are more intelligent than either. They dress in animal furs and tanned hides, and usually carry stone clubs or axes and crude bows. The bows will hit on a roll of 1–3 on one die, for 3 points of damage to their target's STAMINA. Hill Men will usually be encountered on the trail of some prey. They are skilled at tracking down animals, which they then roast on spits above an open fire. They live on boar, deer, wild ducks, rabbits and other creatures. Gathered together in small tribes, they typically dwell in crude grass huts or caves. They don't have

HOBGOBLIN

SKILL: 6
STAMINA: 6
HABITAT: Hills, Dungeons, Ruins, Caves, Wilderness
NUMBER ENCOUNTERED: 1–6
TYPE: Humanoid
REACTION: Hostile
INTELLIGENCE: Average

Possibly the result of interbreeding between Goblins and Orcs, HOBGOBLINS are tall gangling creatures encountered in many wild areas. Unlike Goblins, with whom they will sometimes be living, they are not afraid of sunlight, and make fearsome opponents both above and below ground. They are as tall as men, typically dress in tattered clothes and armour stolen from past opponents, and carry swords or spiked clubs. Like their cousins they revel in torture and death, especially where Elves are concerned. They are ugly, warty-skinned things, and hate anything that is in the slightest way graceful or pretty.

Hobgoblins may be encountered living in primitive settlements in isolated lands, but most of their number serve in the armies of Chaos alongside their inhuman cousins. They are hardy fighters, and may sometimes be encountered leading small companies of Goblins or Orcs into battle. Despite such a rare gift for discipline, they will just as quickly lose it if faced with an Elf or two, and will attack them rabidly without thought for their commands.

grey and black cloth. Above their hunched shoulders they have the rotting heads of rams, complete with large curled horns. Their mouths are flecked with foam, their eyes are a deep red colour, savage but empty, and bare bones poke through ragged clumps of wool and skin. Anyone seeing a Yachar for the first time will immediately lose 2 points of STAMINA because of the revulsion and fear these creatures cause.

Their tasks on their rare visits to the Earthly Plane are to gather the souls of anyone unwise enough to be out on even the most terrible of nights – thieves and assassins, revellers and drunkards. Like most Demonspawn, Yachar can fly (though by magical levitation rather than actual wings). In an attack they will usually swoop down, grab an opponent from behind and try to slash his throat with dagger-length claws (such an attack causes their opponent to defend against this first blow with 3 points off his SKILL).

If a fight starts to go against a Horned Demon, it will cast a Darkness spell over the area, and immediately return to its home plane. Should it win, however, the grisly creature will remove the still-beating heart of the corpse, before returning home to present the fresh soul to its diabolic masters.

HORNED DEMON

SKILL: 12
STAMINA: 9
HABITAT: Ruins, Demonic Plane
NUMBER ENCOUNTERED: 1
TYPE: Demon
REACTION: Neutral–Hostile
INTELLIGENCE: Average

In the stormiest of seasons, on the darkest of moonless nights, HORNED DEMONS roam the lands of men, calling errant souls to hasten to Hell! These foul Demons, also known as Yachar, appear as humans, clad in layers of ragged and mildewed

HOWL CAT

SKILL: 8
STAMINA: 9
HABITAT: Hills, Mountains
NUMBER ENCOUNTERED: 1–3
TYPE: Animal
REACTION: Unfriendly
INTELLIGENCE: Low

When first discovered, HOWL CATS were mistaken for a variety of feline. Indeed, on first sighting, it is not difficult to imagine how this mistake was made. But they were subsequently discovered to be members of the Ape family, even though their heads are more characteristic of a lion than of an ape. They are short-haired apes, about the size of a large dog, and inhabit the timber-line between forests and higher mountainous areas, mainly in the western reaches of Kakhabad. Their bodies are a mottled grey colour, but their heads are ringed with a bold, ruddy mane (hence their resemblance to a lion).

Howl Cats are carnivorous. Though they attack in turn, one after the other, a second creature is rarely needed in a battle. Their jaws are lined with razor-sharp teeth and each hand, or paw, wields a single slashing claw. They take their name from their battle-cry, an ear-piercing shriek which cannot fail to strike terror in the hearts of their opponents. This cry is always a prelude to their launching into attack, and, for the Attack Round following this howl, anyone fighting a Howl Cat must deduct 1 point from their Attack Strength. During a battle, a Howl Cat will voice its cry whenever it takes STAMINA damage, and its opponent must suffer the Attack Strength penalty for the next Attack Round. But each time it utters its scream, this drains 1 STAMINA point from the creature.

HYDRA

	Body	Each head
SKILL:	0	9
STAMINA:	9	5

HABITAT: *Marshes, Ruins, Dungeons, Wilderness*
NUMBER ENCOUNTERED: *1*
TYPE: *Monster*
REACTION: *Hostile*
INTELLIGENCE: *Average*

The HYDRA is a many-headed creature which can unfortunately be found in many different types of terrain. Though they are rare, they often figure as the villains of heroic tales. They are reptilian creatures, like fat-bodied snakes, with a number of large heads rising on long necks from their bodies. The number of heads can be found by rolling one die and adding one, to give the beast between two and seven wide-mouthed, fang-filled heads. A Hydra has as many Attacks as it has heads. Covered in green-brown scales, but usually dripping mud and slime, the nightmarish beasts can grow as much as ten metres long.

Each head has its own brain and can attack separately. In a fight, its opponent can engage one head while defending against the others, each of which has a separate Attack Roll. If its opponent wishes, he can concentrate on attacking the thing's body to kill it outright. He can deliver one automatic hit each round, while defending against all of the heads. Once its body is dead, the heads will also die, flopping to the ground on limp necks.

ICE DEMON

SKILL: 9   *3 Attacks*
STAMINA: 11
HABITAT: *Demonic Plane, Ice*
NUMBER ENCOUNTERED: *1*
TYPE: *Demon*
REACTION: *Hostile*
INTELLIGENCE: *High*

The trappers of the Icefinger Mountains talk in hushed whispers of a certain sheltered valley high in the mountains, from where streams of fanatical Orcs, Goblins and Neanderthals have been known to pour out, to raid trading posts and villages for slaves and sacrifices. The raiders are surprisingly disciplined and it is widely thought that they are ruled over by an evil lord who has trained them. In fact, their leader is a powerful ICE DEMON, called to the Earthly Plane by his devoted acolytes.

For most of the time, the beast simply squats, as motionless as a statue carved from the ice, watching and listening to its worshippers. It can communicate telepathically with the shaman who rules them, ordering attacks or sacrifices as it desires. When a captured human is brought for sacrifice, it is placed inside a magical blue circle carved out of the ice in the floor before the 'Frozen One'. The Demon will come to life and attack, rows of icicles snapping from its limbs as its great body lumbers forwards.

The Ice Demon stands at least six metres tall, and is fat and strong. Its grim head supports two huge, curving ram's horns. Behind it, a wide pair of bat's wings spread for almost ten metres. It is completely white, and appears to be made from the ice itself. In an attack it will wield two massive fists. From its nose and mouth, a freezing vapour will gust, hitting on a roll of 1–3 on one die, and freezing away a further 1 point of STAMINA. Should the Demon be defeated, its evil spirit will be banished back to Hell, and its body will shatter like a block of ice.

When the gullible victim touches the Imitator, he will stick fast, held by a glue-like substance secreted by the creature. At the same time it will strike with a large fist-shaped protrusion. The trapped prey can fight back, but with a SKILL reduced by 2. Once the 'fist' has been cut off, the victim can finish off the Imitator at leisure, before slowly prising himself off the glue.

IRON-EATER

SKILL: 4
STAMINA: 5
HABITAT: Caves, Dungeons, Ruins
NUMBER ENCOUNTERED: 1
TYPE: Monster
REACTION: Neutral
INTELLIGENCE: Low

IRON-EATERS are strange, jelly-like creatures, rather like giant amoebas, which surprise many adventurers by dropping on to them from ceilings and overhangs. If its victim is unaware of it, the thing will land on him on a roll of 1–5 on one die. Otherwise, a normal Attack Round should be rolled. If the Iron-Eater hits successfully, it has landed; if not, it has missed, and can be finished off in one blow on the floor.

IMITATOR

SKILL: 9
STAMINA: 8
HABITAT: Dungeons
NUMBER ENCOUNTERED: 1
TYPE: Monster
REACTION: Hostile
INTELLIGENCE: Low

In dark places underground there lurk strangely malleable creatures called IMITATORS. In their natural form they are shapeless, flowing things, like a pool of thick mud. When hunting their favourite food – warm meat – they can adapt themselves to look like something else. To trap an unintelligent creature they may mimic its potential food; for a more intelligent human or Orc, they will pose as a door or treasure-chest.

Once the creature has struck, it will start to feed, not on flesh, but on the metal of a helmet or breastplate! The strange beast will chew large holes in the armour, removing 1 SKILL point for each item (helmet, shield, breastplate, etc.) that it eats. A normal Attack must then be rolled to remove the Iron-Eater; if the beast wins, it has clung on to its opponent and will destroy another item. If it loses, it will be injured as normal, and will drop to the floor, where it can be finished off.

JAGUAR

SKILL: 8
STAMINA: 7
HABITAT: Jungles
NUMBER ENCOUNTERED: 1–2
TYPE: Animal
REACTION: Neutral–Unfriendly
INTELLIGENCE: Low

JAGUARS are ferocious predatory cats found chiefly in the jungles of the south. They live on smaller creatures such as boar, monkeys and deer, though when they are hungry they will take on creatures much larger than themselves. They will attack any creature they believe is a threat to them – especially man. They are hunted extensively by the primitive jungle tribes for their marvellous pelts, and are very wary of all humanoids as a result. Sometimes, a Jaguar cub will be taken from its jungle home and reared and trained as a pet for someone rich enough to pay the exorbitant price. Like all the big cats, they are difficult to handle, and can never be truly domesticated. Kept fed with a lot of fresh meat and fit with a lot of exercise, though, they make excellent guards, though their loyalty is never as strong as a Dog's, and they have been known to turn on their masters at the slightest whim.

JIB-JIB

SKILL: 1
STAMINA: 2
HABITAT: Hills, Caves
NUMBER ENCOUNTERED: 1–2
TYPE: Animal
REACTION: Neutral
INTELLIGENCE: Low

In the hills of Low Xamen dwell a number of strange creatures, but none more strange, perhaps, than the JIB-JIB. Shy and secretive in the extreme, they look like a tiny ball of fur (no bigger than a cabbage, as one wise sage put it) on two short, stumpy legs. They have small, frightened eyes, set just above a large mouth. Jib-Jibs are vegetarians, living on small bushes and plants, from which they suck the juices and nutrients, since they have neither teeth nor claws.

These timid creatures have evolved an effective defence against the many predators that live off small, harmless beasts like themselves. They have developed tremendously loud voices, with which they begin to howl in an unearthly, ear-splitting wail whenever they feel danger threatening. The din will scare off even the largest of unintelligent creatures and most more intelligent ones too, by tricking them into thinking that they are about to be attacked by a ravening horde of blood-crazed Demons! Only the very bravest (or perhaps the stupidest) of creatures will ignore the horrendous screams and investigate further, to discover the timorous little Jib-Jibs, hiding and shaking in some corner, howling fit to raise the dead!

and eaten. Kokomokoa are particularly enamoured of Elves' flesh, which they consider a great delicacy, and great celebrations are held on the rare occasions when such meat is on their menu after a particularly successful raid! These grisly cannibals have no need of treasure or money, but many keep pretty gems, since they are attracted by their sparkle.

KOKOMOKOA

SKILL: 5
STAMINA: 5
HABITAT: Marshes, Jungles
NUMBER ENCOUNTERED: 3–18
TYPE: Humanoid
REACTION: Unfriendly
INTELLIGENCE: Low

The swamps and jungles of the south-east are home to many strange tribes. One race, known as the KOKOMOKOA, are a major menace to trappers and adventurers in the area. Standing a little over a metre high, these squat, green-skinned humanoids seem reptilian, because of their scaly skin and webbed feet. Their heads are wide and flat, their eyes large and yellow. They can swim well, their long, bony legs propelling them swiftly just below the surface with only their large eyes breaking the water.

Kokomokoa, so called because of their ululating war-cries, live together in compact family groups, in huts woven from rushes and covered in hardened mud. These crude dwellings are very difficult to find, camouflaged as they are to blend with the surrounding vegetation, and act as secure bases from which the tribes mount raids over the area. Sometimes, Kokomokoa will train Giant Marsh Spiders as sentries, to watch over their females and young while the warriors hunt for food.

In an attack, Kokomokoa will often use nets (hitting on a roll of a 1 or 2 on one die), which hold down their prey, while others spear it with their short bamboo javelins (since the nets will temporarily remove 3 points from their captive's SKILL). Once captured, their victims can expect only to be boiled

KRELL

SKILL: 8
STAMINA: 5
HABITAT:
    Wild – Forests, Jungles
    Tame – Towns, anywhere men are
NUMBER ENCOUNTERED: 1–6
TYPE: Animal
REACTION: Friendly–Neutral
INTELLIGENCE: Average

Originally found in the steamy jungle of the east, KRELL are six-armed ape-like creatures. Covered in thick mats of brown hair, they are incredibly nimble, and swing dextrously through the trees at great speeds. In the wild, Krell are very hard to find, since they are very shy creatures, who blend into the thick jungle foliage. They live in small family groups, hunting and eating parrots, rats and other small creatures, as well as fruit and roots.

The quick wits of the Krell make them ideal as pets or magical familiars for wizards and other characters. They are highly suited to sneaking, spying and thieving, as much at home clambering up walls and over roof-tops as they are swinging through trees. In a fight they can be quite vicious, hanging on to their foe with as many limbs as possible, and then biting with sharp, pointed teeth.

Occasionally, their masters will teach them simple tricks, such as juggling or tumbling, and some Krell are dressed in miniature suits of clothes and taught to bow and be courteous. In their natural habitats, Krell communicate in a complicated language of clicks and chatters. A few of their owners learn this language, but none can match the achievement of the Arch-wizard Belandros, who taught his Krell to speak the language of men.

LEAF BEAST

SKILL: 6
STAMINA: 3
HABITAT: Port Blacksand
NUMBER ENCOUNTERED: 3
TYPE: Magical creature
REACTION: Hostile
INTELLIGENCE: Low

Despite his mean reputation, Lord Azzur, the ruler of Port Blacksand, has one passionate love: exotic flowers, which he exhibits in the public gardens. Pride of place in his collection is given to a small crop of the legendary Black Lotus plants. The rarity of these plants is such that the nobleman uses magical guardians to prevent them from being stolen.

Around the bowl containing the flowers stand three bushes, expertly trimmed to look like large animals. Should anyone touch a Black Lotus, the three LEAF BEASTS – lion, tiger and leopard – will spring to life and attack ferociously! A single opponent will be able to match his Attack Strength with all three, but he can injure only one of them at a time. If a hit is indicated on the other two, he has simply held off their attack. When they have dealt with the would-be flower-picker, the beasts will spring back on to their pedestals and turn back into bushes.

GIANT LEECH

SKILL: 1
STAMINA: 1
HABITAT: Marshes, Rivers
NUMBER ENCOUNTERED: 2–7 (1 die plus 1)
TYPE: Animal
REACTION: Neutral
INTELLIGENCE: Low–None

GIANT LEECHES are found among the still, rank backwaters of marshes and swamps across Allansia, Kakhabad and beyond. Disgustingly soft and tube-like, almost half a metre long, they swim leisurely around the brackish creeks, awaiting a warm-blooded creature to feed upon. When one passes, they latch on to it with tiny, hook-like teeth and begin to suck its blood. Each Leech will take 1 STAMINA point of blood a round, up to a limit of 3 points each, before falling off satiated and full of blood. Pulling off a Giant Leech will cause a further point of STAMINA damage, as its teeth tear away a large patch of skin. Striking and killing a Leech with a small knife needs a successful *Test for Luck*, or the blow will miss and cause another point of damage. A safer way to remove a Giant Leech is to sprinkle it with salt, which causes the revolting creature to shrivel up and die.

LEPRECHAUN

SKILL: 10   2 Attacks
STAMINA: 4
HABITAT: Forests, Plains, Caves, Ruins, Dungeons
NUMBER ENCOUNTERED: 1–3
TYPE: Humanoid
REACTION: Friendly–Neutral
INTELLIGENCE: High

Many an adventurer has come to grief at the hands of a group of mischievous LEPRECHAUNS. They are small magical humanoids, at most a metre tall, which delight in playing tricks on unsuspecting people. They will appear out of nowhere, dressed in baggy clothes (usually coloured a dazzling spring green) and chuckling merrily. They may throw a rotten tomato, or just beckon for the person to follow them, laughing all the time in their squeaky little voices. They will lead their new acquaintance to where their fellows lie in wait, ready to play more tricks and hopefully steal some treasure or food.

They can fly, hovering about in the air without the aid of wings, as well as turn invisible at will, conjure up illusions, and so on. If their foolish victims try to attack them, the Leprechauns will simply toss some magic dust in their faces, which will cause paralysis for an hour or more, and give the pests plenty of time to loot as much as they can carry. However, should their victim prove actually to have a sense of humour, and share their jokes (despite being the butt of them), the Leprechauns may become friendly and help him on his way – though they won't return anything they've stolen.

Their eyes are milky white and apparently lifeless, but behind them lies a wickedly cunning intelligence, always full of plans for filling their gullets with fresh meat. Despite their wiry forms and thin, dangling limbs, the Stealers are inhumanly strong. They fly with surprising elegance, using the large pair of feathery wings that sprouts from their shoulders.

Life-Stealers live in large caves high in the mountains, in groups of two or three. It is not known how they reproduce, if at all. No young have ever been seen in a raid, and no one has been able to get anywhere near their lofty homes and return to tell of what they saw there! Some folk-tales, though, say that the Life-Stealers are the warriors of the evil Storm God Sukh, said to dwell in an enormous stone palace high in the clouds above the mountains. Such stories are usually nothing more than rumours, though many of them also point out that some Life-Stealer corpses have been found, after unsuccessful raids, wearing gold pendants in the form of Sukh's traditional symbol – a skull with a circular mouth, as if blowing the wind. Such pendants are extremely rare, and considered highly valuable by many sages anxious to get their hands on one. Most are unable ever to do so. Life-Stealers may be rare, but dead ones are rarer still. When they come soaring down on the thermals from their desolate peaks, broad wings beating together in a rhythm of death, they usually get what they desire – a feast of human flesh.

LIFE-STEALER

SKILL: 12   2 Attacks
STAMINA: 18
HABITAT: Mountains, Caves
NUMBER ENCOUNTERED: 1–2
TYPE: Monster
REACTION: Hostile
INTELLIGENCE: Average–High

Not even sages record a name for these creatures more specific than simply LIFE-STEALERS. Certainly, for the mountain tribes who live in constant fear of their attacks, no other name is necessary. Flying out from their lairs high in the peaks, they wreak havoc on isolated farmsteads and small villages in their quest for human food.

Life-Stealers are tall, thin humanoids with sinewy, leathery bodies. Their heads are long and thin, the skin stretched taut across the skull. Their ears are wide and almost bat-like, and they have short tusks which spill from a mouth brimming with teeth.

LIVING CORPSE

SKILL: 6 (see below)
STAMINA: 6 (see below)
HABITAT: Ruins, Dungeons
NUMBER ENCOUNTERED: 1–3
TYPE: Undead
REACTION: Hostile
INTELLIGENCE: Average

In the violent lands of Kakhabad and Allansia it is not uncommon to stumble across the scene of a battle, with fresh corpses left sprawled on the ground where they died. But when some of the bodies begin to rise to their feet, a clever man will realize that no ordinary battle took place there, as the LIVING CORPSES ready themselves to attack their next victim!

Similar in appearance, if not in manner, to Zombies, these ghastly beings look like half-decayed bodies, the flesh falling away in places to reveal internal organs and bare bones. Their rotten state makes them seem fairly fragile, but they can move surprisingly fast for a dead body! They will leap on their alarmed opponent and try to strangle him with their bony, flesh-peeling fingers.

Should their opponent manage to land a hit on a Living Corpse, the creature will split up into six separate parts, and each will attack its victim, biting, clawing, crushing, kicking and hitting without respite. The parts are as follows:

Dice roll	Part	SKILL	STAMINA
1	Head	3	1
2	Body	2	1
3	Left arm	3	1
4	Right arm	3	1
5	Left leg	2	1
6	Right leg	2	1

Each part will attack separately with its own Attack Strength. Each roll should be checked against the opponent's single Attack Strength. For each one that is higher, a hit will be delivered to the victim. For his part, he can attempt to hit only one of the parts (chosen at random by rolling one die on the table above). If his attack is better than the part's, he

will put it out of action and it will not attack him again. However, the body part will stay in the fight, and he may accidentally hit it again, wasting a blow. If a single Living Corpse is facing more than one opponent, it will divide its parts between them. Should every part finally be defeated, they will flap ineffectually until they reunite into their true form again – a battered (and now really dead) corpse.

GIANT LIZARD

	Adult	Young
SKILL:	8	5
STAMINA:	9	5

HABITAT: Hills, Forests, Plains, Deserts
NUMBER ENCOUNTERED: 1–2
TYPE: Reptile
REACTION: Unfriendly
INTELLIGENCE: Low

Six metres long and one and a half metres high, ferocious GIANT LIZARDS can be major hazards to adventurers in many parts of Allansia and northern Kakhabad. Huge versions of their smaller cousins, they roam far and wide in search of fresh meat. The creatures appear slow, as they lumber along on four ungainly feet and drag their cumbersome tails behind them, but in a fight they prove to be remarkably agile, darting beneath swords to deliver savage bites from their large fang-filled mouths.

Giant Lizards are solitary, aggressive reptiles as a rule, but they will meet up once a year to mate, producing a clutch of one to three eggs, before parting again. Young Giant Lizards will hatch out in twelve weeks or so. If trained from birth, Giant Lizards can be made to carry a rider, and as a result their eggs fetch a high price. It is believed that both the Lizard Men of Fire Island and the Caarth of the southern deserts maintain large troops of cavalry mounted on Giant Lizards.

LIZARDINE

SKILL: 8
STAMINA: 8
HABITAT: Towns
NUMBER ENCOUNTERED: 1
TYPE: Humanoid
REACTION: Neutral
INTELLIGENCE: High

No one is really sure where LIZARDINES come from. Different scholars talk of a hidden kingdom beyond the eastern jungles, of an isle in the southern seas, or of a mysterious land across the western oceans. The scaly humanoids will appear as if out of nowhere, stay for a few years, and then move on as if they had never been there at all. They look a little like Dragons, but with a human's proportions rather than a lizard's – longer arms, straighter legs and no wings. They are covered in scaly skin, usually a deep red colour, though in keeping with human conventions they will wear a few clothes or wrap themselves in a cloak.

If encountered in a town, a Lizardine may well be discreetly running a shop, selling strange magical trinkets from far-away lands. The most common of these are scorpion-shaped brooches of different metals which will bring luck, strength or protection to their wearer, but they may also sell other items too. Such treasures occasionally attract foolish thieves, who are unaware that the Lizardine has its own defences. In an attack the beast can breathe fire from its mouth, which will hit its target on a roll of 1–3 on one die, causing 1 point of STAMINA damage in addition to any normal fighting damage caused by its claws. Such abilities have sometimes caused frightened townspeople, fearing the beasts, to drive them out of their settlements. Because of this, the Lizardines are discreet and secretive, keeping to themselves as much as possible, and basing their businesses in the merchants' quarter of a town or port, where they are lost among the many other bizarre and foreign inhabitants.

LIZARD KING

SKILL: 9   2 Attacks
STAMINA: 10
HABITAT: Jungles, Marshes, Ruins, Dungeons
NUMBER ENCOUNTERED: 1
TYPE: Reptile/humanoid
REACTION: Hostile
INTELLIGENCE: High

As little as five centuries ago, what is now the great race of Lizard Men was little more than a few disorganized tribes who spent most of their time fighting or eating one another. From them, though, have come the LIZARD KINGS, superior reptilian beings who have taken control of the race, and begun to organize it into a civilization. Each tribe is now ruled over by a Lizard King, each of whom in turn pays fealty to the members of a grand council of the wisest and strongest beasts, in the creatures' capital in the southern swamplands. Lizard Kings are taller and stronger than normal Lizard Men, and far more intelligent. They are civilized and sophisticated, in their own way, and are great leaders.

Protected at all times by a guard of twenty hand-picked Lizard Man warriors, they are nevertheless superb fighters themselves, their favourite weapons being magical fire-swords. According to custom, the Lizard King race keeps itself as separate as it can from the lowly Lizard Men, and interbreeding is punishable by death, to ensure that their race is kept pure.

LIZARD MAN

	Lizard Man	Two-headed Lizard Man	Mutant Lizard Man
SKILL:	8	9	9
STAMINA:	8	10	9

HABITAT: *Jungles, Marshes, Ruins, Dungeons*
NUMBER ENCOUNTERED: *1–6*
TYPE: *Reptile/humanoid*
REACTION: *Hostile*
INTELLIGENCE: *Average–High*

There are some areas of this world where man will never rule. The vast swamps and jungles south of the Desert of Skulls are not inhospitable by any means, but they are securely controlled by LIZARD MEN. These evil reptilians are strong and warlike, and seek always to extend their dominion. Thankfully they need a warm, moist climate to survive; the nearest colony is on Fire Island off the Skull Coast of southern Allansia.

The green-skinned Lizard Men stand up to two and a half metres tall, and their bodies are covered in tough, scaly skin. They are like fat humans with a lizard's head and a long tail. A ridge of spikes runs up their backs, and two horns project from the top of their heads. They will usually be dressed in skilfully fashioned armour, and carry one of a number of weapons, such as a scimitar, spear, sword, axe or whip. They are fairly clever creatures, divided in rank throughout their vast armies according to experience and intelligence. These armies are well trained and equipped, for they are led by a separate race of superior Lizard Men known as the Lizard Kings. They hoard gold and precious metals, and set all their captives to work at digging for them in their mines.

Lizard Men have managed to train various reptilian species for use as riding-animals, for no horse will bear them. Giant Lizards are used most often, for they are quick and nimble-footed over rough terrain. They are not very strong, however, so Styracosauruses are also used. These are harder to train, for they are exceptionally stupid, but they are very strong, and ideal for smashing a path through an enemy's ranks.

The race is a Chaotic one, and has a number of rare sub-species as a result. TWO-HEADED LIZARD MEN are often found serving as priests, for their more normal relations seem to regard them as being blessed by their Gods. (Lizard Men worship a whole host of reptilian Deities, including the savage Lizard God Suthis Cha, and the Snake Demon Myurr.) They are larger and crueller than their more normal cousins, and are allowed free rein to slaughter slaves and prisoners as the mood takes them, for they serve the Gods and their actions are never questioned.

Less fortunate are MUTANT LIZARD MEN, who are despised for their more irregular deformities, and as a consequence tend to form the front line in battles. They may have twisted limbs, lumpy bodies, a different skin colour, hunched backs, or one or more of a hundred other mutations. When sacrifices to the Gods are in short supply, they may end up as unwilling participants in appeasement rites, as their two-headed cousins despise them most of all, on the grounds that the things blaspheme against the purity of the reptilian race with their ugly, twisted bodies.

MAMMOTH

	Adult	Young	
SKILL:	10	7	2 Attacks
STAMINA:	16	10	

HABITAT: *Ice, Plains*
NUMBER ENCOUNTERED: *1–6*
TYPE: *Animal*
REACTION: *Unfriendly*
INTELLIGENCE: *Low*

MAMMOTHS are huge shaggy-haired beasts, similar to elephants, but dwelling chiefly in cooler climes. They are rare creatures, encountered most frequently on the barren northern plains around the Icefinger Mountains, but a few scattered herds have been reported in other icy areas. They are usually coloured a deep brown, with large curving tusks extending out in front of them. They are fairly docile, and wander in small herds in search of vegetation to feed upon. Mammoths are also rather stupid, and a whole herd can take fright from the threatening movements of a much smaller creature. There will be a larger male Mammoth with most herds, however, who will valiantly attack to defend his cows and calves. In an attack, a bull Mammoth will rear on its back legs, brandishing its tusks threateningly, and attempt to knock over and trample its enemy.

Mammoths are hunted by many of the northern tribes, both humans and Toa-Suo, for their meat, ivory and warm shaggy pelts. Folk-legends told by the shamans of such tribes tell of when the plains were greener and the Mammoth roamed everywhere. Such times are long gone, for the plains are now desolate and grey, and the Mammoth are being hunted into extinction.

MAN-ORC

	Adult	Young
SKILL:	8	4
STAMINA:	6	3

HABITAT: *Towns, Forests, Hills, Plains*
NUMBER ENCOUNTERED: *1 or 2–12 (see below)*
TYPE: *Humanoid*
REACTION: *Neutral–Unfriendly*
INTELLIGENCE: *Average–High*

The sorry mongrel offspring of Orcs and humans, MAN-ORCS are shunned by both races. They look very much like humans, but much uglier, with large teeth and ears and ruddy-brown skins. They may be found living alone in towns or the countryside, but in more isolated areas there are small farming villages of Man-Orcs, such as Torrepani in the Shamutanti Hills. Man-Orcs are unfriendly towards humans, for most of them remember beatings and stonings at their hands. Orcs despise them and treat them as worthless slaves to be whipped and abused, and eventually cast out or even killed. As a result Man-Orcs live a lonely existence, scraping a living out of the earth, well away from other beings who might harm them.

MANTICORE

SKILL: 12   3 Attacks
STAMINA: 18
HABITAT: Ruins, Caves, Dungeons, Wilderness
NUMBER ENCOUNTERED: 1
TYPE: Monster
REACTION: Hostile
INTELLIGENCE: Average

MANTICORES were created centuries ago by an insane warlock from beyond the Western Ocean, fooling with things that should have been left well alone. Using powerful magic, he mixed a lion, scorpion and a bat together with a human and created the first Manticore. He repeated the experiment many times, until he was finally killed by one of his creations. Since then the monstrosities have scattered into the most inhospitable parts of the world, where their evil natures fester with hatred for all life.

A Manticore has the head of an old, bearded man, which flows into the mane and then the body of a huge lion. From their powerful shoulders a pair of large, leathery bat's wings sprout, and behind them rears a scorpion-like tail tipped with a sting the size of a man's head! They will attack with their claws or their sting, alternately slashing and striking at their opponent. After a successful hit, a roll of 5 or 6 on one die indicates a hit from its poisoned sting rather than its claws, causing 6 points of damage, unless its opponent can avoid it by a successful *Test for Luck*. Their slashes will otherwise do the usual 2 points of damage.

In a Manticore's lair there will be innumerable bones, the sorry relics of its past victims. There may also be some weapons, equipment or treasure, for it cannot digest such hard items.

MANTIS MAN

SKILL: 6
STAMINA: 5
HABITAT: Forests, Plains, Hills
NUMBER ENCOUNTERED: 1
TYPE: Humanoid
REACTION: Neutral–Unfriendly
INTELLIGENCE: Average

The so-called MANTIS MEN of the northern Baklands have, in their isolation, developed an alarming method of ensnaring their food. When first encountered, a Mantis Man will invariably be standing totally motionless, more like a life-sized statue than a real being. Its long arms and hands will be raised to its chest, clasped together as if the 'statue' were praying devoutly! A wary creature may spot a blink of an eye, or a tremble of the hands, before the Mantis Man's arms shoot forward to grab its prey. A Mantis Man can be fought normally, but if at any time it delivers a successful strike on its opponent, it will lift and kill him instantly with a bite from its wide, fang-filled mouth. A victim's only hope, therefore, is to try to damage its arms and render it unable to attack.

In the wild, Mantis Men live alone or in small groups. When out hunting, though, they will always be on their own – even the stupidest creatures may get suspicious of a whole tribe of motionless statues! Mantis Men are attracted to bright and shiny things, and will often hoard any such items found on their victims.

MARSH HOPPER

SKILL: 4
STAMINA: 4
HABITAT: Marshes
NUMBER ENCOUNTERED: 1–3
TYPE: Humanoid
REACTION: Friendly (see below)
INTELLIGENCE: Average

Related to the Kokomokoa of the south-eastern jungles, MARSH HOPPERS are small amphibian humanoids which dwell in the marshes of Fire Island and western Allansia. Standing about one and a half metres tall, they have large heads, with huge, almost sad eyes and wide mouths. Their bodies are small in comparison, and covered in green scales. Their arms are long and very dextrous, their legs shorter and ending in wide,

webbed feet. Cunning in the extreme, they know the marshes backwards, and will often appear to aid lost adventurers. However, they will really lead them into the lairs of larger monsters such as Slime Suckers or Hydras in return for a few left-over scraps of meat. Marsh Hoppers live in small, isolated family groups, hidden deep in the swamps well away from larger predators. The nimble creatures often roam far and wide across the marshland, however, searching for a suitable meal. They usually live on fish, frogs and other small creatures, but their cunning minds occasionally bring them a far richer feast!

MARSH WRAITH

SKILL: 7
STAMINA: 5
HABITAT: Marshes, Rivers
NUMBER ENCOUNTERED: 2–7 (1 die plus 1)
TYPE: Monster
REACTION: Unfriendly
INTELLIGENCE: Low

In the dark, fetid creeks and backwaters of slow-moving rivers and marshland, danger sometimes lurks, ready to catch adventurers unawares. Man is not lord over every domain; in some areas, older, darker beings hold sway. MARSH WRAITHS are strange, primal creatures, related to Earth Elementals, and dwell in the still waters among the head-high reeds. They spend much of their time wallowing in the mud, lazily sifting insects into their mouths. They are very territorial creatures, and will tenaciously defend their patches against any intruders who would disturb them.

Should they sense the vibrations of approaching creatures through the water and rushes, Marsh Wraiths will rise from the swamp as one. When solidifying for an attack, they form themselves into a vaguely humanoid shape, dripping with slime. They will try to warn off the trespassers in a sombre moaning voice that has given many men the impression that they are some strange form of undead being (hence their name). If warnings do not deter the intruders, they will attack, all at once, in a coordinated assault that belies their low intelligence, and try to smother their opponent in mud. Because of their insubstantial forms, hits on them will only do 1 point of STAMINA damage. If a Marsh Wraith is very severely injured, it will retreat by dropping back into the mud and swimming away under the surface of the water.

Little is known about the life-cycle of a Marsh Wraith. Smaller creatures have been encountered, but sages have been divided over whether they were females, immature young, or just smaller than normal. One theory is that the creatures reproduce by dividing themselves into separate Marsh Wraiths, each instantly able to carry on living as normal. It is not thought that they keep any possessions; their slimy forms would not be able to grasp any treasure long enough to appreciate it.

Medusa will attempt to trick him into gazing into its sickly red eyes. Anyone failing a *Test for Luck* will be caught by its stare, and cannot turn away. His limbs will begin to stiffen and within a few moments he will be nothing but solid stone! If its intended victim is swift enough to cover his eyes, the Medusa will approach and allow its snakes to lash out and bite him. Fighting the Medusa with eyes closed, slashing from side to side with a sword, temporarily reduces the opponent's SKILL by 2 points. If, by some chance, the Medusa's prey is carrying a mirror or some other reflective device like a polished shield, the Medusa may look into it. A *Test for Luck* is required for such a chancy manoeuvre; if it succeeds, the vile creature will transmute into rock and crumble to dust in an instant.

MEDUSA

SKILL: 6
STAMINA: 5
HABITAT: Ruins, Caves, Dungeons
NUMBER ENCOUNTERED: 1
TYPE: Humanoid
REACTION: Hostile
INTELLIGENCE: Average

To many unfortunate adventurers, there appeared nothing dangerous about the bent old woman, her head covered by a thick shawl. Most offered to help her, drawing near to lend a strong arm to steady the poor old crone. And then she threw back her shawl and fixed them with a red-eyed stare, and they were lost . . .

A MEDUSA is a strange humanoid that looks much like a wizened old lady dressed in ragged clothes. However, in place of normal hair there sprouts a mass of wriggling snakes! It usually dwells in isolated ruins or caves, well away from other creatures, but ventures out occasionally to search for prey. When it encounters a choice human, the

MERMAN

	Merman	Mermaid
SKILL:	7	4
STAMINA:	10	7
HABITAT:	Sea, Lakes	
NUMBER ENCOUNTERED:		

Merman – 1–6
Mermaid – 1
TYPE: Fish/humanoid
REACTION: Neutral–Unfriendly
INTELLIGENCE: High

MERFOLK are, quite simply, the people of the sea. They may once have been human, but their bodies are now perfectly adapted to life under the waves.

Their upper halves are as normal humans, except that they have a pale blue-green tint. They have air-breathing lungs, but there are also gill-slits in the sides of their neck, usually hidden by their long flowing hair. From the waist downwards, though, each has a tail like a fish, covered in scales. They can swim very fast using their tails, yet still carry weapons or objects in their hands. They make their homes in caves and sheltered corners on the ocean floor, where they grow crops of seaweed, algae and other food.

The MERMEN are the warriors of the race. Proud and haughty, they may sometimes be seen patrolling the depths with dolphins, on the look-out for sharks or other predators. They will usually be carrying spears or tridents, and sometimes shields. They have no time for the affairs of the surface world, and will treat the infrequent humans they encounter with disdain.

The females of the species, the MERMAIDS, have a different view of the world beyond the waters. A lone Mermaid may sometimes be met basking on a rock in a secluded part of the sea-shore, singing to herself. The song of a Mermaid is so enchanting that all males who hear it will immediately fall in love with her. She will choose one of them, and beckon him into the water with her. The chosen person will desperately want to do this, but may *Test for Luck* to see if all his resistance is overcome. In this case, if he is Unlucky, he will resist the Mermaid's song, her spell will be broken and she will swim away alone. If her victim has been charmed, and no one tries to stop him, they will dive beneath the waves together to live under the sea. In time, his body will adapt until he becomes a Merman, and the Mermaid will come looking for another human.

MESSENGER OF DEATH

SKILL: 7
STAMINA: 6
HABITAT: Demonic Plane, anywhere their victim is
NUMBER ENCOUNTERED: 1
TYPE: Magical creature
REACTION: Neutral
INTELLIGENCE: High

When one is in need of an assassin, there are many highly trained men available for hire. But when one has a particularly skilled or stubborn enemy to eliminate, only a MESSENGER OF DEATH will do. These fell creatures can be summoned from one of the Demonic Planes by a secret ritual to kill powerful opponents, taking as payment the life-force of their victim.

They appear as Zombie-like humans, dressed in ragged shrouds, their eyes and mouth full of mucus which makes their voice little more than a sickly gurgle. They silently approach their victim, tap lightly on one shoulder, murmur 'Death!' in a most dramatic manner, and then slink away to lay out the traps for the game which will follow. The Messenger will stay ahead of its victim, leaving letters marked in prominent places – painted on doors, chipped into stone and so on. If all the letters are read, they will spell the word 'Death', and the Messenger will reappear to watch the life drain out of its helpless prey.

Messengers can only be harmed at the very moment the 'contract' is finalized, when the word is first spoken. As the vile creature touches its victim to seal it, its guard is dropped, and a silver dagger plane and negate the contract.

MIK

SKILL: 12
STAMINA: 7
HABITAT: Ruins, Dungeons, Towns
NUMBER ENCOUNTERED: 1–3
TYPE: Humanoid
REACTION: Neutral–Hostile
INTELLIGENCE: High

There is probably less known about the strange race of Elf-like humanoids called MIKS than any other beings. They are very rare, appearing without warning in a group of perhaps two or three, before departing again as if they had never been there. Worse, Miks are masters of illusion, able to transform themselves into any shape or form they desire. As a result, few have seen them as they really are – pale, emaciated humanoids with large, intelligent heads.

A Mik's mastery of illusion is astounding. If it is disguised as a venomous snake, for example, and bites someone, he will die from the bite! They cannot, for some reason, simulate or use metal in their disguises, however, and their illusions cannot be cast over other objects or beings. They are a highly mischievous and aggressive race, and delight in playfully killing anyone they meet. They love gold, though, and can sometimes be bribed into letting someone go free. If threatened with violence, they will respond with their favourite weapon, a needle-knife (a thin stiletto-like dagger), or just turn into a bird and fly away!

MINOTAUR

SKILL: 9   2 Attacks
STAMINA: 9
HABITAT: Dungeons, Ruins
NUMBER ENCOUNTERED: 1
TYPE: Humanoid
REACTION: Hostile
INTELLIGENCE: Average

According to tradition, at the heart of every good labyrinth there is a MINOTAUR. This perilous beast is half-man, half-bull – a fearsome combination. Its head is shaggy and bovine, with a huge pair of horns curving from the top. Its body is muscular and covered in short hair. Its overall colour is sandy brown, though it will be filthy with dust and muck. It can use weapons, if it has them, but its favourite method of fighting is a head-down charge, snorting and stamping just like a bull. Minotaurs may sometimes be placed to guard their master's treasure-hoard, though they are more often the final trap at the heart of a deadly maze.

MIRROR DEMON

SKILL: 10   2 Attacks
STAMINA: 10
HABITAT: Demonic Plane, Dungeons
NUMBER ENCOUNTERED: 1
TYPE: Demon
REACTION: Hostile
INTELLIGENCE: Average

In the lower Demonic Planes all natural laws are suspended and bizarre beings dwell in several dimensions at once. Sometimes they will slip between gaps in space and time, and materialize on the Earthly Plane to trap some choice humans to torment. MIRROR DEMONS are horrific humanoid beings with four arms and four faces that scream wildly. They are always encountered close to a large mirror, which is their doorway back to their own dimension.

It is highly intelligent and has many ingenious tactics for ensnaring its prey. It lives on the life-forces of any creatures it can catch, chilling them by swathing them in its arms, before sucking their souls from their bodies with wispy fingers. It usually feeds off frogs, lizards and marsh birds, wafting over them and freezing them before they know they are dead. Sometimes, however, it gets to feast on larger, more satisfying sustenance, such as a man.

The Demon will try to grab hold of its victim with its clawed hands and pull him into the mirror. Should its opponent lose an Attack Round, he will find himself drawn through into the Demon's dimension, from which he will never escape. Smashing the mirror requires a strong, steady blow, which is not easy when a screaming monstrosity is clawing at you! To smash the mirror the Demon's opponent must roll his SKILL or below on two dice. If this happens, the Mirror Demon's lifeline will be destroyed and it will die. However it is killed, cracks will begin to race across its face and body, and it will collapse with an ear-splitting crash into a small pile of shattered glass.

Its favourite lure is to leave a conspicuous item of treasure or equipment, the remains of some previous victim, in a prominent position on the pathway some distance ahead of an approaching victim. When he arrives at the spot, the Mist Vampire moans and calls for help a little way off, from among the mists. It will lead its victim out into the marsh until he is lost, and then attack. The creature can only be hit by magical weapons; others pass straight through its ghostly body! On a successful hit, instead of inflicting the usual damage, it will remove 1 point of SKILL from its opponent with its chilling touch. Should the victim's SKILL reach 0, he will die. The Mist Vampire will take the last dregs of his soul, and allow his drained, lifeless body to sink slowly down into the marsh . . .

MIST VAMPIRE

SKILL: 8
STAMINA: 9
HABITAT: Marshes
NUMBER ENCOUNTERED: 1
TYPE: Magical creature
REACTION: Hostile
INTELLIGENCE: High

MIST VAMPIRE is the name given in the tales of the marsh people to a strange, ghostly creature said to dwell deep in the inaccessible reaches of the marsh. Related to Will-o'-the-Wisps, it usually appears amid the shifting mists and fogs of its home as a pale, vaguely man-shaped spirit, wavering like a spectre over the rushes.

MUCALYTIC

SKILL: 8   2 Attacks
STAMINA: 9
HABITAT: Dungeons, Towns (sewers)
NUMBER ENCOUNTERED: 1–2
TYPE: Monster
REACTION: Unfriendly–Hostile
INTELLIGENCE: Average

Well known in folk-tales for their disgusting habits, MUCALYTICS are vile, slime-loving things. Vaguely humanoid in shape, but about the size of a bear, they are lumpy, ugly beasts. Most of their features are hidden under the filth and muck they plaster over themselves, but the trunk-like snouts that poke from the front of their faces will be visible, snorting the air or rooting in the slime. They are revolting beasts, and anyone encountering them in their cesspool of a lair will immediately lose 2 points of STAMINA as a result of the stench.

In a fight, a Mucalytic will flail about with its huge arms, but when it has softened up its opponent, it will resort to other tactics. After landing three successful blows, the Mucalytic will grab hold of its opponent, draw him near to its mouth and breathe on him. A Mucalytic can exhale highly poisonous fumes at will, of which even a short sniff is enough to kill!

No one is sure where the disgusting beasts came from, but it is well known that the Archmage in Mampang hired some to guard his dungeons. It is said that they still lurk beneath the citadel, wallowing in their slime and filth.

MUDCLAWS are small, two-legged amphibians which dwell in small colonies among the thickets of reeds and rushes on the fringes of marshes and river-banks. Standing only half a metre or so tall, they are coloured in mottled patterns of green and brown blotches, which provide them with good camouflage against larger predators. They have powerful legs with wide, webbed toes, allowing them to both run and swim at high speed. They have a high ridge of bony spikes across their backs, and a short tail which helps them steer when swimming. Their short arms finish in surprisingly strong prehensile hands, which are equipped with short, sharp claws.

Mudclaws will eat almost anything they can find, including fish, insects and plants, but are most fond of warm-blooded meat. They will take rats, voles and stray herd animals, and will occasionally gang together to assail lone adventurers. Many an unwary traveller has suddenly found himself being assaulted on all sides by the ravenous little beasts, slashing and rending with dagger-sharp claws, trying to drag him into the water before tearing off strips to eat. In such a coordinated attack, they can be more deadly than Piranhas, though smaller groups tend to be less blatant and more selective in their choice of meals.

The creatures live in dens similar to those built by beavers, small hut-like structures of woven reeds covered with mud and grass. Their young cannot provide for themselves until almost fully grown, relying instead on the food brought by their intriguingly loyal parents.

MUDCLAW

SKILL: 5
STAMINA: 4
HABITAT: Marshes, Rivers
NUMBER ENCOUNTERED: 4–14 (2 dice plus 2)
TYPE: Animal
REACTION: Unfriendly
INTELLIGENCE: Low

MUMMY

SKILL: 9   2 Attacks
STAMINA: 12
HABITAT: Ruins, Dungeons
NUMBER ENCOUNTERED: 1
TYPE: Undead
REACTION: Hostile
INTELLIGENCE: Low

In musty crypts and tombs some corpses grimly hang on to a semblance of life, almost as if they were afraid to let go and die. In countries where the dead are embalmed and wrapped tightly in bandages to be preserved these undead beings appear as MUMMIES. They can move only slowly, as they are wrapped in constricting bandages, but they can unerringly find living creatures, detecting their life-forces like a beacon in the darkness.

They attack by flailing about with their fists. Fighting a Mummy is not as straightforward as it seems, for they cannot be truly killed by blows from weapons. Although they will appear to die, they will return to life after twenty minutes and follow their would-be killers, to extract revenge. The only sure way of finishing off a Mummy is to set it on fire. Even a single touch with a blazing torch is sufficient for its bone-dry wrappings to catch fire and completely immolate the Mummy in a few seconds, leaving nothing but a pile of ashes.

They attack in packs and must be fought as a single creature, adding 1 SKILL and 3 STAMINA for each additional Mungie in the pack. The creatures have glowing red eyes and have the advantage of night vision.

As plants are attracted towards the sun, Mungies are uncontrollably drawn towards Gold. They are the ultimate natural pickpockets, using their nimble reactions to pilfer Gold from the packs or even the pockets of any adventurers whose concentration wanders. They prefer to steal at night, when there is less chance that they will be spotted. Anyone asleep in a Mungie area will without doubt fall foul of their thievery. In fact, anyone walking through Mungie territory even in broad daylight will have to *Test for Luck* to see whether the Mungies are successful.

But apart from this lust for Gold, Mungies are quite harmless and will attack only in self-defence. An adventurer may only attack them (i.e. will only be able to follow their quick movements) if he has a SKILL of 10+ at night or 9+ during the day. Anyone with a lesser SKILL will just not be able to catch the little creatures.

More unscrupulous adventurers have often wondered whether it would be possible to train a Mungie to steal Gold for their own purposes. In fact this *is* possible, but no one has so far succeeded. Only a wizard would be able to capture one of the little creatures and then cast a Control Creature spell.

MUNGIE

SKILL: 5
STAMINA: 4
HABITAT: Mountains, Hills
NUMBER ENCOUNTERED: 3–5 (1–3 on 1 die, plus 2)
TYPE: Animal
REACTION: Unfriendly
INTELLIGENCE: Low

Similar in appearance to Wraith Apes, but somewhat smaller, MUNGIES appear in packs of three to five. They move with lightning-quick reactions.

NANDIBEAR

SKILL: 9   2 Attacks
STAMINA: 11
HABITAT: Caves, Hills, Wilderness
NUMBER ENCOUNTERED: 1
TYPE: Monster
REACTION: Hostile
INTELLIGENCE: Low

Somewhere between a bear and an ape, and larger than either, the NANDIBEAR is a brutal, solitary beast found only in isolated regions. It is carnivorous, its favourite food being human flesh (especially the brains!). Despite its great size, it can move very quietly, since soft pads on its great clawed feet soften its tread. When it attacks from behind, it will surprise its opponent, and automatically cause 2 points of STAMINA damage with its powerful claws. After this first attack the fight will proceed as usual.

A Nandibear will often make its lair in a cave or hollow in the rocks, where it will return with food it has caught. The lair will be full of bones and half-chewed meat, but little treasure, for the Nandibear has no need of it and clears it from its home regularly.

It is somewhat alarming to note the number of supernatural creatures, sent by various Deities, that can be found following a particularly heroic adventurer. The Gods of Good send the Suma to ease their path to glory. The Trickster Gods of Luck and Chance set mischievous Genies in their path to tempt them with wishes and false advice. And the nameless Gods of Evil that the Demon Princes follow will dispatch the perilous beings known as NANKA.

Like Genies and Suma, this magical creature has no material form. When it wishes to appear to another being, it will manifest as a vague humanoid formed from thick black smoke in which a pair of dark eyes glint wickedly. Usually, however, a Nanka will set up a trap to ensnare its victim and bring his soul to its terrible masters. A favourite trap involves the Nanka hiding inside a glass phial, which is left where its prey is sure to find it. When the flask is unstoppered, the thing will flow out as a cloud of smoke and envelop the adventurer. It will then flow back into the phial, taking its unfortunate prey with it, and replace the stopper by magic. Once it has captured its victim, the Nanka will transport him to the Magical Planes and deliver his soul for its masters to feed upon. Only magical weapons can offer any defence against the malevolent Nanka.

NANKA

SKILL: 12
STAMINA: 20
HABITAT: Magical Planes, anywhere their victim is
NUMBER ENCOUNTERED: 1
TYPE: Magical creature
REACTION: Hostile
INTELLIGENCE: High

NEANDERTHAL

SKILL: 7
STAMINA: 8
HABITAT: Ice, Wilderness, Hills, Caves
NUMBER ENCOUNTERED: 1–6
TYPE: Humanoid
REACTION: Neutral–Unfriendly
INTELLIGENCE: Low

The brutish semi-humans known as NEANDER-THALS are a primitive and violent race to be found in many areas. They will usually be encountered as a hunting-party or in a settlement – typically a crude circle of huts around a religious totem or statue. They look like thin, filthy humans, with wild hair and untrimmed claw-like nails on their hands and toes. They will be carrying crude spears and knives, and may be decorated with poorly made pendants, bracelets, and studs in their ears and noses.

They are unintelligent beings and will sometimes be found in the service of a cleverer leader – an Orc, Goblin, or maybe even an evil human. Neanderthals have a whole pantheon of primitive Gods, for they worship everything they don't understand from the sun to a mountain. One member of a tribe may be a shaman, dressed up with bones, feathers and rattles and covered in bizarrely painted designs. They have no special powers except a great sense of theatre and ritual. Anyone demonstrating real magic to a Neanderthal tribe can expect to be treated as nothing less than a God!

NIGHT DEMON

SKILL: 14
STAMINA: 18
HABITAT: Demonic Plane, Ruins, Dungeons
NUMBER ENCOUNTERED: 1
TYPE: Demon
REACTION: Hostile
INTELLIGENCE: High

Huddled around their foggy scrying-pool, the mists flowing about their vast shadowy halls, the four NIGHT DEMONS keep a close watch on the affairs of men. The Princes, named Kalin, Relem, Shakor and Vradna, are the tacticians of the Legions of Hell, directing demonic forces to wherever they are needed. Occasionally one of them will appear on the Earthly Plane in person, to oversee the latest stage in their struggle against the forces of Good.

The Night Demons stand almost three metres tall, but the almost tangible aura of power which surrounds them makes them seem even taller. They have human bodies, thickly muscled and tanned a deep red-brown colour. Their hands and feet are covered in tough lizard-like scales, and end in sharpened claws. They have two heads, black and dragon-like; each contains half their intelligence, but can talk and think independently of the other, which can be highly confusing when all four Princes argue at once. The Demons can fly, using their large, bat-like wings, but more often travel in large, skull-encrusted chariots drawn by hundreds of Demonic Servants.

If encountered on the Earthly Plane, they will often manifest as the evil mastermind behind some foul human cruelty. Their powers of persuasion are immense, and many villainous men take orders direct from them. They have other powers too. In common with many Greater Demons, they can only be injured by weapons that have been enchanted or blessed; holy water and other pure items can repel them like a cross does a Vampire. Out of the palms of their hands they can project bolts of flame once a day, which will hit an opponent on a roll of 1–3 on one die, causing two dice of damage. In close-up combat they will use their hands another way, slashing at an opponent with their cruel claws. If such a blow is successful, it will cause 3 points of STAMINA damage. Worse still, a Night Demon's spirit cannot be killed on this plane, though its temporary earthly body can be destroyed. Its three brothers will call it back to Hell, where its true body lies awaiting its return. A Demon so banished cannot return to earth again for sixty-six days; once it has regained its powers, however, it will pursue its enemy without respite, until it has exacted a revenge fitting for a Demon Prince.

NIGHT STALKER

SKILL: 11   2 Attacks
STAMINA: 8
HABITAT: Dungeons, Caves
NUMBER ENCOUNTERED: 1
TYPE: Humanoid
REACTION: Hostile
INTELLIGENCE: Average

In the dank, forbidding depths of dungeons deep below the ground, many perils stalk the darkness in search of their next meal. The NIGHT STALKERS were perhaps human once, but they are something less than human now. Bent over from their endless wanderings in the oppressive tunnels, they are sinewy beings, covered in folds of leathery grey skin. Their facial features are gruesome – eyes sunk deep into sockets and permanently squinting, teeth as long as a man's little finger, skin wrinkled and warty. Their arms are long and thin, and end in large, clawed hands that can split stone or skulls with equal ease. They may be carrying a small lantern to guide their unceasing patrols, and they may wear pretty, worthless trinkets stolen from past victims for the nice way they sparkle in the wan lantern light.

N'YADACH

SKILL: 6
STAMINA: 8
HABITAT: Ruins, Caves, Dungeons
NUMBER ENCOUNTERED: 1–6
TYPE: Humanoid
REACTION: Unfriendly–Hostile
INTELLIGENCE: Low

The ancient legends of the Dwarfs speak of a subterranean race of evil humanoids, and of the terrible wars that raged across the centuries as the two proud peoples strove for dominance of the underground kingdoms. Called the N'YADACH, they were fearsome warriors, backed up with dark sorcery, and won many battles. In time, however, the superior troops and war-machines of the Dwarfs, aided by a rebellion of their enemies' slaves, the Skorn, brought about victory, and the power of the N'yadach waned.

Nowadays there are very few remaining members of the once proud race, dwelling in small clans in isolated caves and burrows. They have forgotten much of their past skills and are rather sorry creatures. They are as tall as men when stood fully upright, but their lives underground have left them stooped and hunched. Their heads are long, almost Wolf-like, with ears pressed back along their skulls. They have small, cat-like eyes, which can see very well in the poorest light and are backed up by a keen sense of smell. They have two poisonous fangs which protrude from the sides of their mouths. They are thin, covered in short grey hair, which is tattered and unkempt, and have long, muscular arms and short legs that end in clawed feet.

N'yadach typically wear a few scraps of armour, and carry clubs reinforced with iron bands. They live on any food they can find on their wanderings, usually rats and mosses. They communicate in a guttural, snarling language that has lost all past refinements, and they can no longer read or write their ancient script. N'yadach breed but rarely, and this, together with their harsh lifestyle, means they are fast dying out, the last sorry remnants of a once proud race.

GIANT OCTOPUS

SKILL: 9   *4 Attacks*
STAMINA: 10
HABITAT: Sea, Caves
NUMBER ENCOUNTERED: 1
TYPE: Mollusc
REACTION: Unfriendly
INTELLIGENCE: Low

Over cups of strong rum in the taverns of ports the length of the land, wizened old sea-dogs tell tales of gigantic sea-monsters which have attacked all sorts of ships from fishing-smacks to war-galleys. Closer to the land, such creatures are smaller, but just as perilous. Lurking in caves and pools along the coast, GIANT OCTOPUSES can sometimes be encountered. Growing to quite alarming sizes, the creatures are cunning predators, with strong, dextrous bodies. They will attack and feed upon most living creatures, typically anchoring themselves on a rock with two sucker-lined tentacles and lashing out with the others.

Their favourite tactic is to grasp a creature, gradually enfold it in their tentacles and crush the life out of it. Should a Giant Octopus score two successful hits in succession, without taking any in return, it will have grasped its opponent tightly and will squeeze him for a further point of damage. Unless its victim can break the hold by scoring a successful hit on the creature in return, the crushing damage will increase by a further point each time. Should the hold be loosened, the Giant Octopus can start trying to score two successive hits again, and so on, until one of the combatants is dead. Should the Octopus find itself the victor, it will drag the corpse of its victim beneath the water to be dismembered and eaten at leisure.

OGRE

SKILL: 8   2 Attacks
STAMINA: 10
HABITAT: Hills, Plains, Forests, Towns, Caves
NUMBER ENCOUNTERED: 1–6
TYPE: Humanoid
REACTION: Hostile
INTELLIGENCE: Average–High

Large, ugly and violent, OGRES are foul humanoids related to Orcs, Goblins and Trolls, and a whole host of cross-breeds. The average Ogre, if there is such a thing, stands about two metres tall, though the race is so Chaotic that this can vary up to a metre either way. They are very ugly to look upon, their savage faces lumpy and bestial, and drooling spittle everywhere. Ogres are strong creatures, more than a match for most men, and very skilled with their crude clubs and axes.

In the wild, Ogres lead solitary lives in isolated caves away from civilization. These more primitive beings dress in animal skins, and live by hunting. They will attack almost anything or anyone they encounter with surprising ferocity.

These days, however, many Ogres are more civilized, if that is the right word, and serve in the armies of evil sorcerers or noblemen. These Ogres will be trained and equipped for fighting, with battle-axes, war-hammers and even bows, and may be encountered in bands of up to six. Despite such new sophistication, though, Ogres are still crude and violent by nature, and delight in the torture and death of smaller beings.

ORC

	Common Orc	Great Orc
SKILL:	6	7
STAMINA:	5	6

HABITAT: Plains, Towns, Wilderness, Dungeons, Ruins, Caves
NUMBER ENCOUNTERED: 1–6
TYPE: Humanoid
REACTION: Hostile
INTELLIGENCE: Average

On one side there are the forces of Good – humans, Elves and Dwarfs. On the other there are the forces of Evil – Goblins, Ogres, Trolls and ORCS. Of all the noxious inhuman creatures an adventurer must overcome during his quests for fame and fortune, Orcs will always be the most frequent of his adversaries. Orcs infest almost everywhere, though they prefer dark underground regions: like Goblins, they dislike sunlight. They are squat, ugly brutes, shorter than a man, but taller than a Goblin. They have warty brown-green skins, usually covered in a motley assortment of skins, furs and irregular scraps of armour scavenged from previous opponents. Their favourite weapons are serrated swords, whips, flails, morning stars and spears.

Orcs are disgusting, filthy creatures with vile habits to match. They delight in the pain of others, even weaker members of their own race, and they will torture their captives before setting them to work as slaves. The living-quarters of an Orc stronghold will be knee-deep in filth and muck, and will be very unhealthy, to say the least. Orcs delight in unsavoury activities. Their favourite food, for example, is a rare dish called Elf intestines in Gnome's-blood sauce, though when this is out of season they have to settle for more mundane delights like rat-gizzard soup, or curried bat surprise.

The armies of the Orcs are led by GREAT ORCS. Larger and stronger than common Orcs, they are possibly the result of selective breeding with Trolls. If more than four Orcs are encountered, one of them will be a Great Orc. If one is present, it will keep the rest from squabbling and brawling with one another. Orcs are argumentative beasts, who seem to spend more of their time fighting among themselves than against the dreaded Elves and Dwarfs.

Like all the Chaotic races, some unfortunate Orcs are mutants, with an amazing assortment of deficiencies. They may have strange skins, elongated or shortened limbs, or special powers, such as flying, telepathy and so on. Most mutants are despised by more normal Orcs, who treat them as if they were slaves, or mangy dogs suitable only for kicking and beating.

GIANT OWL

SKILL: 6
STAMINA: 7
HABITAT: Hills, Plains, Forests, Ruins
NUMBER ENCOUNTERED: 1–2
TYPE: Bird
REACTION: Neutral
INTELLIGENCE: Low

GIANT OWLS are rare creatures, because they avoid harassment by inhabiting very remote areas. In the past, many princes and lords kept the birds for hunting and as status symbols, and as a result few are now left in the wild. These magnificent birds stand up to one and a half metres tall, with a wingspan of almost double that. Like their smaller cousins, they are usually nocturnal, emerging at sundown to hunt for food in the twilight. Giant Owls usually feed upon sheep and goats, preferring herd animals to humanoids who might fight back.

These birds make their homes at the tops of large trees, and occasionally in ruined towers and the like. Their nests are like those of any bird, built from twigs and branches, woven together and lined with feathers and down. A pair of Giant Owls will produce a clutch of one or two eggs only once a year. Their eggs and chicks fetch exorbitant prices from noblemen, as the young can with care be trained like hawks, some even to be ridden! The parents tend to be wary to the point of aggressiveness, if they feel that their brood is being threatened. Giant Owls attack in high-speed dives which add 4 to their SKILL for their first attack. Their talons are cruelly sharp, and can easily slice through helmets and shields.

PEGASUS

SKILL: 12   2 Attacks
STAMINA: 12
HABITAT: Magical Plane, Mountains
NUMBER ENCOUNTERED: 1
TYPE: Animal
REACTION: Friendly
INTELLIGENCE: High

The PEGASUS is a magical winged horse, always the purest white in colour, which is seen only rarely in this world. It dwells mostly on the Magical Plane of Air, though it will sometimes be encountered in the remotest of mountains high above the clouds, where it can live without disturbance. Shy creatures, they can be summoned by someone with a good heart by the promise of silver. For such a gift, they will carry a passenger anywhere he wishes to go. They are very strong and can fly at great speed. They are also highly intelligent, but speak only the languages of aerial creatures. If danger threatens, they can fight with their hoofs if necessary, but will normally just blink back to the Magical Plane and safety.

PHANTOM

SKILL: 12
STAMINA: 2 (see below)
HABITAT: Ruins, Dungeons
NUMBER ENCOUNTERED: 1
TYPE: Undead
REACTION: Hostile
INTELLIGENCE: High

Just the sight of a PHANTOM stalking through the night, hidden in its voluminous black cowl, its ghostly lantern swinging ahead of it, is enough to scare any faint-hearted being to death. Those brave enough actually to challenge the godless being will encounter the full extent of its power as it throws back its hood and reveals its face. A Phantom is a powerful undead spirit, usually found inhabiting a deathless human body. Its skin is stretched taut across its bones, a sickly yellow in colour. Its eyes trap attention: blood-red and sunk into their sockets, they can paralyse those who meet their powerful gaze.

Anyone looking into the eyes of a Phantom must roll his current SKILL score or less on two dice, or lose 4 STAMINA points and be paralysed for fifteen minutes. The Phantom will use this time to make good its escape, fleeing away to continue its haunting elsewhere. If its opponent manages to survive the gaze and wishes to fight it, he will have another shock, for the thing is unaffected by blows from normal weapons. As soon as its opponent misses, or the weapon passes straight through its body, the Phantom will catch his gaze in its own again, and he will be paralysed. The only hope is to use a silver implement, for the very touch of an object made from this metal will cause the undead being to crumble to dust, its roving spirit finally released to return to the Spirit Plane in peace.

PIRANHA

SKILL: 6
STAMINA: 1 (see below)
HABITAT: Lakes, Rivers
NUMBER ENCOUNTERED: 2–12
TYPE: Fish
REACTION: Hostile
INTELLIGENCE: Low

PIRANHAS are found in the rivers and lakes of the hot southern jungles, where they are greatly feared. They are voracious feeders, and can strip a horse to the bone with their teeth in a few minutes! Each fish is between twenty and thirty centimetres long, but they always swim and feed in a pack. The first sign most swimmers have of their presence is a turbulence in the water, as though it were boiling and bubbling, before they are jostled and buffeted as the Piranhas fight one another to be the first to feed. The pack can be treated as having a single SKILL, with each fish having a STAMINA of 1. There are few tactics one can use against Piranhas: having a piece of fresh meat to distract them is useful, but few swimmers will be carrying such a thing!

PIT FIEND

SKILL: 12   3 Attacks
STAMINA: 15
HABITAT: Jungles, Plains, Deserts
NUMBER ENCOUNTERED: 1
TYPE: Reptile
REACTION: Unfriendly
INTELLIGENCE: Low

Whether it is the descendant of a long-dead Dinosaur, or a Giant Lizard that has learnt to walk upright, the PIT FIEND is a frightening creature. Standing close on ten metres high on two enormous clawed legs, it is covered in a tough leathery hide mottled with blotches of green and brown. Its head is large, with powerful jaws designed solely for snapping bones and rending flesh, for the beast is utterly carnivorous. Its name comes from its use in games, where gladiators chosen from condemned prisoners are sent into a huge pit to fight one of the brutes, much to the delight of a bloodthirsty audience.

GIANT PITCHER-PLANT

	Tendril	Vase
SKILL:	8	0
STAMINA:	7	11

HABITAT: Jungle
NUMBER ENCOUNTERED: 1–2
TYPE: Plant
REACTION: Neutral
INTELLIGENCE: None

Standing almost three metres tall, the GIANT PITCHER-PLANT looks very much like an enormous vase, covered in vines and creepers. Like many other plants around it in the depths of the jungle, it has evolved to many times the size of normal pitcher-plants. These particular plants are quite rare, but can prove a hazard to anyone exploring deep in the jungle.

Pitcher-Plants are carnivorous, living off any large creature they can capture. A strong, whip-like tendril, almost seven metres long, extends from the lip of the vase. Should any creature disturb the sensitive carpet of vines around the vase's base, the tendril will attack. If it scores a successful hit, it will wrap itself around the target and lift it into the vase to be digested. Unless the victim can finish off the tendril in the very next strike, he will find himself down inside the plant, in a metre of stagnant rainwater.

The inside of the plant is covered with sharp spines to prevent anything climbing out again. Should a creature try to escape, it will suffer 15 points of STAMINA damage before reaching the lip. Once the plant has deposited its food into the vase, it will secrete digestive acids into the water that will do 1 point of damage every minute until the food is dissolved. These acids are not strong enough to harm most metals, so the inside of a vase may contain quite a hoard of treasure. The inside walls of the plant are toughened, to withstand the acid, and cannot be damaged. Anyone attacking the outside, however, can free a victim once the body of the plant has been killed. Hits on the vase are automatic, but only if the tendril has been destroyed. Every three blows will take one minute; once the vase is destroyed, the acid will flow away, and the victim can be rescued – if he is still alive!

PIXIE

SKILL: 5
STAMINA: 5
HABITAT: Forests, Plains
NUMBER ENCOUNTERED: 1–3
TYPE: Humanoid
REACTION: Friendly–Unfriendly
INTELLIGENCE: High

PIXIES are tiny, delicate humanoids, usually encountered in areas well away from humans, who seem to enjoy tormenting the little beings. They are peaceful creatures who care for nature and natural things. Pixies stand about half a metre tall, and are typically dressed in human-style clothing of browns or greens. They live together in small villages hidden away in the countryside. Here they tend their crops and generally live a contented life away from larger beings. Occasionally, however, they may be encountered elsewhere, perhaps in the villages of Dwarfs or in open country.

Pixies don't automatically loathe humans – they are far too well mannered – but they will be very wary of any they meet unless they prove to be genuinely friendly. They will avoid starting a fight with a larger being, for they know it would be suicidal for them. Nevertheless, if set upon, they will defend themselves as best they can with their short knives. Should they ever encounter a Sprite, however, they will waste no time in setting about it. Perhaps they are jealous of the wings and magic powers of Sprites; at any rate, Pixies will always fight the unfortunate creatures to the death.

POLTERGEIST

SKILL: 9
STAMINA: 0 (see below)
HABITAT: Ruins
NUMBER ENCOUNTERED: 1
TYPE: Undead
REACTION: Hostile
INTELLIGENCE: Average

Ancient folk-tales sometimes claim that victims of a particularly violent murder will remain at the place of their death, unable to depart from the Earthly Plane until their killers themselves die. Such spirits may manifest as POLTERGEISTS. They are spiteful and malevolent, and will try to harm anyone entering their domain. They are invisible and immaterial, and cannot physically attack their opponent. Instead they will throw chairs, plates, rocks and other small objects. To avoid such a missile, their opponent must successfully *Test for Luck*, or suffer 1 point of STAMINA damage. The Poltergeist may even try to wield a stick or a weapon (in which case its SKILL score should be used for the fight). Fighting a Poltergeist is rather futile, however, as it cannot be hit by weapons. The only hope for its opponent is a fast retreat out of the spirit's range!

PYGMY

SKILL: 6
STAMINA: 5
HABITAT: Jungles, Forests
NUMBER ENCOUNTERED: 2–7 (1 die plus 1)
TYPE: Humanoid
REACTION: Neutral–Unfriendly
INTELLIGENCE: Average

In some parts of the world primitive tribes of semi-humans still live, cut off from civilization. In remote jungle areas, stunted savages known as PYGMIES dwell. A little over a metre tall, they wear only loincloths, and their skins have been turned dark brown by the sun. They live on fruit and roots, as well as monkeys and other small creatures, which they hunt with blowpipes and poisoned darts. The venom is not strong enough to kill a human,

but it will knock someone unconscious if it hits him (3 in 6 chance). Each dart will also cause 1 point of STAMINA damage.

Pygmies love gold and jewellery, and will steal it from their unconscious victims before melting back into the jungle. They live in well-hidden villages deep in the undergrowth, ruled over by a tribal chief and his witch-doctor. In the village there will also be between three and eighteen females and between two and twelve children, none of whom are able to fight.

GIANT RAT

SKILL: 5
STAMINA: 4
HABITAT: Ruins, Dungeons, Towns (sewers)
NUMBER ENCOUNTERED: 2–7 (1 die plus 1)
TYPE: Animal
REACTION: Unfriendly
INTELLIGENCE: Low

GIANT RATS are a menace to all those who would search for treasure in ancient ruins or tombs. They are just like normal rats, but much larger – about a metre long, with sharp claws and teeth that can gnaw through plate armour. They tend to hunt in small packs, of which one Giant Rat will usually be the leader. Larger and stronger than the others (add 1 point to both SKILL and STAMINA), it will appear to be giving orders to them via a complicated language of squeaks. If the leader is killed – a difficult task since it will try to remain at the rear in any fight – the other Giant Rats will retreat in disorganized panic, allowing their opponents to escape safely.

RAT MAN

SKILL: 5
STAMINA: 6
HABITAT: Ruins, Dungeons, Towns (sewers), Caves
NUMBER ENCOUNTERED: 1–6
TYPE: Animal/humanoid
REACTION: Unfriendly
INTELLIGENCE: Low

Alchemists and sorcerers have long laboured to create hybrid creatures to serve them as warriors and slaves. Many such experiments have been in cross-breeding men with hardier species. Some have worked well, but others have produced weak, regressive breeds like the RAT MEN.

A little over one and a half metres tall, they have the bodies of humans, but the heads of rats, with big eyes and ears, sensitive whiskers and large front teeth. They are covered in short, soft fur, and they have long rat-like tails. Rat Men dress in humans' clothing, and can speak their language, but are otherwise shunned, made outcasts by their appearance. They have long been banished to sewers and old ruins in the wastelands, where they dwell in small groups, catching and eating anything they can. Despite their weakness, Rat Men are dextrous and have become skilled with snares, traps and slings. They can track well, sniffing the air to pick up a scent. They will try to strike from a distance, for they are not so skilled with their shortswords, preferring to use them only when finishing off a trapped prey prior to eating it.

RAZORJAW

	Adult	Young
SKILL:	10	6
STAMINA:	12	5

HABITAT: *Volcanic areas*
NUMBER ENCOUNTERED: *1–2*
TYPE: *Monster*
REACTION: *Hostile*
INTELLIGENCE: *Low*

The RAZORJAW makes its nest among the foul sulphur pools and boiling mud around volcanoes; such a volatile and nauseous habitat suits the vile creature admirably. Over four metres long, they are slimy, reptilian monstrosities with ungainly, leathery bodies and stubby limbs. Their long, scaly necks support eyeless heads with great mouths lined with sharp teeth. The beasts are not affected by their blindness at all, for they have such an inbuilt hatred of all life that they can attack unerringly. From the very moment it bursts out of its huge, strangely shaped egg, a young Razorjaw knows only that it is hungry, and that it hates! Thankfully, Razorjaws are very rare, and will only ever be encountered in inaccessible volcanic areas, where they can wallow and thrash in the foul pools of mud, sulphur and steam.

RED-EYE

SKILL: *6*
STAMINA: *4*
HABITAT: *Towns, Plains, Hills*
NUMBER ENCOUNTERED: *1–6*
TYPE: *Humanoid*
REACTION: *Unfriendly–Hostile*
INTELLIGENCE: *High*

RED-EYES are thin, spindly humanoids distantly related to Elves and humans; they live in small numbers in many border towns and villages across the semi-civilized world. They are arrogant beings, who delight in harassing and playing tricks on their neighbours as excuses for starting a fight. Anyone caught up in such antisocial behaviour must be on his guard, for Red-Eyes have a deadly natural weapon.

Most of the time a Red-Eye will walk about with its eyelids closed tight to seal in its powerful vision. Their eyes can shoot out deadly bolts of energy when opened, so they have to keep them hidden, for fear of incinerating everything they gaze upon. The strength of their eyes is such that they can make out vague outlines through their closed eyelids. As a result, Red-Eyes are not very accurate in combat. Any time a Red-Eye receives a wound, however, it will let fly with its heat vision. The first shot will be very inaccurate, and can be avoided by rolling 1–5 on one die. Should the Red-Eye be injured again, it will let loose another blast, avoidable by rolling 1–4 on one die, and so on until the blast hits automatically. Each time it hits, the blast burns for one die of STAMINA damage; if a Red-Eye's vision hits the same person twice, he will die.

Because of this power, Red-Eyes are greatly feared and are invariably forced to travel from settlement to settlement, without being allowed to stay in one place more than a single night. As a result their clothes are nothing more than rags and their possessions are meagre – but their hatred for humans grows ever stronger.

RHINO-MAN

SKILL: 8
STAMINA: 9
HABITAT: Plains, Ruins
NUMBER ENCOUNTERED: 1–3
TYPE: Animal/humanoid
REACTION: Neutral–Unfriendly
INTELLIGENCE: Average

The RHINO-MEN of the southern plains are thought to be the sorry remnants of evil experiments by a mad sorcerer many centuries ago. They are huge, bulky humanoids, resembling a cross between a rhinoceros and a human. Their heads are large, with a huge horn of matted hair projecting from their foreheads. Their skin hangs in thick folds, and is tougher than leather armour. If encountered in the wild (a fairly rare occurrence, as they are not a common species), they will usually be on the trail of game, and carrying crude spears and knives. Some Rhino-Men, however, may be found serving as guards and soldiers for an evil leader, in which case they will be carrying better weapons and may be wearing the livery of their master. They don't make particularly good soldiers, for they are surly and clumsy, but their strength serves them in good stead in a fight.

ROCK DEMON

SKILL: 10   3 Attacks
STAMINA: 13
HABITAT: Demonic Plane, Hills, Mountains
NUMBER ENCOUNTERED: 1
TYPE: Demon
REACTION: Hostile
INTELLIGENCE: None

Not all Demons are as sophisticated and decadent as Night or Snake Demons. There are some which are completely without the least vestiges of intelligence – vast brutes whose sole enjoyment comes from swatting, crushing and squashing lesser beings. ROCK DEMONS are particularly brutish. About four metres high, they take the form of ugly, misshapen humanoids equipped with hands the size of a Storm Giant's head! They appear to have a hide made completely of stone which somehow flows and bends like flesh, and can be pierced by a sharp blade. Their legs disappear down into the soil as if it were water. They are violent and aggressive, and delight in killing anything they encounter.

It has been suggested by those brave enough to make a study of the Greater Demons that Rock Demons were originally made by the Princes in mockery of the Earth Elementals. Certainly they bear many resemblances, but their power is nowhere as strong. Despite their size and apparently rocky hides, Rock Demons can be harmed by normal weapons, and they cannot move real stone or earth except to throw at an opponent. Nevertheless, they are more than a match for most as they rise out of the ground, dripping mud and soil, to tower thunderously above their prey.

ROCK GRUB

SKILL: 7   2 Attacks
STAMINA: 11
HABITAT: Dungeons, Caves
NUMBER ENCOUNTERED: 1
TYPE: Insect
REACTION: Unfriendly
INTELLIGENCE: Low

Deep below the surface, monstrous insects chew their way through rock and stone. ROCK GRUBS are enormous creatures, looking like beetle-headed worms. They bore vast tunnels, eating everything in their path with enormously powerful mandibles, and leaving only a sticky trail of slime behind them. They are completely blind, but they appear to be able to sense the heat of living creatures. They are attracted to warmth, and will attempt to eat any living things they encounter, grasping them in their jaws and crushing them before digesting them. Dwarfs sometimes follow Rock Grubs as they burrow through the ground, for they know that the creatures can uncover seams of precious metals, ready to be mined.

SABRE-TOOTHED TIGER

SKILL: 11
STAMINA: 8
HABITAT: Hills, Forests, Caves
NUMBER ENCOUNTERED: 1
TYPE: Animal
REACTION: Neutral–Unfriendly
INTELLIGENCE: Low

SABRE-TOOTHED TIGERS are highly dangerous but luckily rare predatory cats, which dwell in warm, hilly regions. They live on just about any fresh meat they can catch, usually deer and wild boar, attacking with claws and the long fangs which give the beasts their name. Despite their voracious appetites and violent manner, Sabre-toothed Tigers are highly sought after by human hunters, as well as cavemen and other humanoids, for their magnificent pelts, which can fetch as much as 1,000 Gold Pieces in a large town. Among many of the primitive hill-tribes, a chief is chosen by a contest involving the single-handed capture, killing and skinning of a Sabre-toothed Tiger. The pelt is then proudly worn by the new chief, as an unmistakable badge of his office.

SAND DEVIL

SKILL: 10
STAMINA: 7
HABITAT: Deserts, Caves
NUMBER ENCOUNTERED: 1
TYPE: Monster
REACTION: Neutral–Unfriendly
INTELLIGENCE: Low

The sufi (or holy men) of the nomadic tribes of the Desert of Skulls tell many tales of the mysterious SAND DEVILS. Encountered only rarely in the sands of the vast desert wastes, they appear as dense, swirling spirals, shifting and dancing in the heat. They are solitary creatures, but occasionally serve, for the sake of mutual friendship, as lookouts and magical familiars for desert Elves, feeding off the energy cast in their ritual spells.

Sand Devils appear to be wardens over the desert in much the same way that druids care for plants and forests. As a result, they are very territorial, and will try to keep all trespassers away from the areas they care for. They will rise out of the dunes, swirling angrily at the transgressors of their sacred reaches, spitting sand and dust into the air. They fight by enveloping their opponents in abrasive sand, which stings and cuts into flesh, cloth and even metal. Their shifting, insubstantial forms are difficult to strike with any great force; any hit on a Sand Devil will do only a single point of damage.

Water, if thrown over a Sand Devil in sufficient quantity, acts as a virulent poison, and will kill it in minutes. In the rare cloudbursts that bring much-needed water to the parched desert, the creature burrows deep into the dunes, mingling with the sand until the fatal rain passes by.

GIANT SANDWORM

	Adult	Young	
SKILL:	10	7	Adults have 5 Attacks
STAMINA:	20	9	Young have 3 Attacks
HABITAT: Deserts			
NUMBER ENCOUNTERED: 1			
TYPE: Monster			
REACTION: Hostile			
INTELLIGENCE: Low			

The sand rises in a long line as though something were swimming just beneath the surface. Suddenly, the sand is broken and the GIANT SAND-WORM rears in the air, poised to strike. Adult Sandworms can grow to twenty metres long (young ones perhaps half that); their bodies are divided into hundreds of segments that gradually taper towards their tails. Their rudimentary heads are made up of a gigantic oval mouth, lined with a ring of spiky teeth and surrounded by a number of scent glands which enable them to detect their prey. If an adult Sandworm scores two hits in succession on its target, it will swallow him and he will quickly die in the powerful digestive acids in its stomach.

The desert nomads sometimes hunt the Giant Sandworm, using harpoons just like a whaler, while perched astride a horse. The meat from a Sandworm is fairly edible, its teeth can be used to make strong ivory daggers and its skin is very tough and ideal for making tents.

GIANT SCORPION

SKILL: 10   2 Attacks
STAMINA: 10
HABITAT: Caves, Deserts, Wilderness, Ruins
NUMBER ENCOUNTERED: 1
TYPE: Insect
REACTION: Unfriendly
INTELLIGENCE: Low

GIANT SCORPIONS are fearsome creatures found in many parts of the world, from temperate wastelands to the burning hot sands of deserts. They are aggressive predators, and are not afraid of attacking humans. Around three metres in length, they are covered in shiny black or brown armour. Their huge claws extend out on strong limbs, and above their backs hangs their deadly sting, as large as a man's head.

Their typical tactic is to grasp their victim with a dextrous claw and lash him with their sting. Each claw can attack independently; if it is taking on a lone prey, it will attack with both of them at once. If a Giant Scorpion gets a strong grip on its opponent (if 22 is rolled for its Attack Strength or, in the case of two opponents, if both Attacks are successful), its sting will whip forward and inject a fatal poison that will take scant seconds to kill the victim(s). Once its prey is dead, the Giant Scorpion will drag the fresh corpse into its bone-littered cave or a shady corner, and eat it.

SENTINEL

	Gem Sentinel	Metal Sentinel
SKILL:	11	12
STAMINA:	9	12
HABITAT: Among a treasure-hoard		
NUMBER ENCOUNTERED: 1		
TYPE: Magical creature		
REACTION: Hostile		
INTELLIGENCE: Low		

There are many methods employed by wizards and noblemen to protect their vast treasure-hoards, including Golems, Crystal Warriors and SENTINELS. First created by a sorcerer in the service of Baron Kognoy of Kaypong, a province to the east of Fang, they are powerful, near-invisible guardians, though unlike many are quite easy for their master to control. They are created by pouring a specially formulated magical potion over a piece of gem or metal, in order to create a Sentinel of the same basic material. The potion-covered item, typically a Gold Piece or a small damond, will retain its form until touched by human flesh. When creating a Sentinel, it is very advisable to wear gloves!

The potion-drenched object is usually secreted near the top of the treasure it protects, where it will hopefully be picked up by a thief. Once touched by human hands, it will immediately transform into a large, fearsome warrior. The Sentinel cannot be harmed by blows from normal weapons, unless its opponent is in contact with a piece of the material from which it was formed. Thus, to damage a Gold Sentinel its opponent must be holding a Gold Piece, or some other golden item. Should it be defeated, a Sentinel will instantly change back into its original form.

SERPENT GUARD

SKILL: 10
STAMINA: 10
HABITAT: Wilderness, Deserts
NUMBER ENCOUNTERED: 1–3
TYPE: Reptile/humanoid
REACTION: Hostile
INTELLIGENCE: Average

In their labyrinthine stone cities hidden deep in the far southern reaches of the Desert of Skulls, the Caarth are ruled over by demonic sorcerers. Forever searching for ways of extending the powers of their snake forefathers, and in worship of their most beloved Sith, they have tried to merge humanoids with snakes in many ways. SERPENT GUARDS are thought to be the result of one of their more successful experiments.

They are disconcerting beings, with their humanoid upper torso perched above a huge snake's body and tail. Their heads are distinctly snake-like too, with large eyes and wide fang-filled mouths. They are covered with reptilian scales, though their upper quarters are more usually hidden under layers of armour. Serpent Guards are intelligent enough to be given complex orders by their evil masters, usually being assigned to patrol the outer defences of their cities or lands. They will always be carrying an array of weapons, for they are highly skilled in the use of sword, battle-axe and spear, and will prove to be deadly adversaries.

SERPENT QUEEN

SKILL: 9   2 Attacks
STAMINA: 7
HABITAT: Port Blacksand
NUMBER ENCOUNTERED: 1
TYPE: Humanoid
REACTION: Neutral–Unfriendly
INTELLIGENCE: High

The SERPENT QUEEN is a curious being, the subject of much speculation by learned scholars. She arrived in Port Blacksand many years ago, in the company of a merchant who claimed to have found her wandering aimlessly while he was crossing the fringes of the Desert of Skulls. She in turn claimed to have originally been human, but to have been transformed in a cruel ritual by the wicked sorcerer-priests of the Caarth, in a city hidden deep in the desert. In an attempt to resurrect the spirit of an ancient queen, the vile beings had turned her head into that of a snake. Before they completed the ritual, she managed to escape, only to wander across the desert for many days, until she was found.

She now dwells in Port Blacksand, under the patronage of Lord Azzur, who keeps her surrounded with such finery that she is now known as the Serpent Queen. She is a sorry thing, with a quick and violent temper. Anyone who deals with her must guard his tongue, or she may attack him in rage. Her neck will extend from its coils and she will try to sink her poisoned fangs into his neck. Her powerful venom will cause 4 STAMINA points and 1 SKILL point of damage. Rumours in the taverns whisper that she has killed many retainers, and that Lord Azzur would pay well to have her transformed back into a human once more – but no one has yet dared to take up the challenge.

Its features become reptilian, all green and scaly, and spines burst through the clothes down the length of its back to where a long tail now swishes in expectation of the meal to come. Its limbs thicken and it grows taller and broader, its sinewy body surmounted by a lizard-like head, a long forked tongue flicking languidly between alarmingly large teeth. It will attack by slashing with its clawed hands.

Once it has eaten its fill of its prey, the Shapechanger may steal fine items of clothing to replace those ruined by its transformation, before moving on in search of more food.

SHAPECHANGER

SKILL: 10   2 Attacks
STAMINA: 10
HABITAT: Forests, Plains, Hills, Wilderness
NUMBER ENCOUNTERED: 1
TYPE: Humanoid/monster
REACTION: Neutral–Hostile
INTELLIGENCE: High

There are some predators that use stripes or spots to hide in cover until they can leap on their prey. But the SHAPECHANGER has the best camouflage of all, for it can transform itself into other creatures. In the guise of a weak, defenceless being, it will approach its human victim before striking!

Its powers are thought to be part illusion and part physical transformation. It can change the general shape, size and features of its body, and fills in the finer details with a magical illusion rather like hypnotism. It mostly takes the form of a small, weak creature such as a Goblin, a Pixie, or even an ageing human – anything that will enable it to get close to its prey. Once it is in range, the Shapechanger's appetite will ruin its concentration, and it will begin to change back into its natural form.

SHARK

SKILL: 7
STAMINA: 6
HABITAT: Sea
NUMBER ENCOUNTERED: 1–3
TYPE: Fish
REACTION: Hostile
INTELLIGENCE: Low

SHARKS of all types may be found in the warm waters of the southern half of the Western Ocean, where they roam constantly in search of food. They can prove a great hazard to swimmers and sailors, and are able to hear movement in the water from over a mile away. Once blood is spilled, the water will soon be full of hungry Sharks, hoping for an easy kill. For every wound inflicted, either on a Shark or its opponent, there is a 1 in 6 chance that another will arrive and attack the creature that was injured. Fighting underwater is difficult, and will temporarily remove 2 points from a land-dweller's Attack Strength. There is also the danger of drowning. Unless an opponent can defeat the Shark(s) in less rounds than his current SKILL, he will drown and become a meal for the Sharks anyway.

Although Sharks are normally found in the sea, they may also be encountered as part of a nasty trap in a dungeon or tomb. They will be much the same as ocean-dwelling Sharks, but in this case others will not be attracted by the smell of spilled blood.

SKELETON

	Skeleton	Skeleton Warrior
SKILL:	6	8
STAMINA:	5	6

HABITAT: Dungeons, Ruins
NUMBER ENCOUNTERED: 1–6
TYPE: Undead
REACTION: Hostile
INTELLIGENCE: Low

SKELETONS are the favourite servants of many evil sorcerers. They are fairly easy to animate, like Zombies, but unlike the latter they do not fall apart after a few months. They are not intelligent, but they will be bound obediently to their master, who can give them short commands up to about twenty-five words long. If their master dies, the Skeletons he animated will instantly fall apart. They are fairly skilled at fighting, not least because their jerky, almost insect-like movements distract their opponents. They will typically be armed with swords or axes. Since they are nothing more than bones held together with a little magic, swords and daggers have great trouble harming them. Anyone using an edged weapon will cause only 1 point of damage to a Skeleton. Smashing and crushing weapons will do normal damage.

Some necromancers have managed to instil a greater fighting skill into their Skeletons, to create SKELETON WARRIORS. These will usually be clad in strong armour and carrying a broadsword or battle-axe. Again they need short commands, but since they are unable to do anything but fight, the orders can be more specific. They are usually left on guard-duty over particular areas, patrolling unceasingly until they encounter an intruder. Skeleton Warriors are like normal Skeletons in that sharp weapons only do 1 point of damage to them; blunt weapons do normal damage.

SKORN

SKILL: 5
STAMINA: 5
HABITAT: Dungeons, Caves
NUMBER ENCOUNTERED: 2–7 (1 die plus 1)
TYPE: Humanoid
REACTION: Neutral–Unfriendly
INTELLIGENCE: Average

> First came N'yadach, cruel master of all.
> Then crept lowly Skorn, forever in thrall.
> But rebellion's fire burnt palace and hall,
> And sore-abused servants brought on their
>   downfall.
> – Ancient Dwarfish rhyme

In times gone by, the SKORN were enslaved by the N'yadach and were set to build elaborate underground palaces for their cruel masters. But war came, an endless, costly war against the Dwarfish nations, and the Skorn were put to work building siege-engines instead. They worked until they dropped, and were then whipped until they rose again. The Skorn were typically patient, thoughtful creatures, but, sweating away in the darkness, they plotted to overthrow their evil captors. A major offensive by the Dwarfs provided them with a distraction: they killed their guards with daggers secretly made from flint, and threw off their chains. Their chambers were soon overrun by the Dwarfs, with whom they joined forces to cleanse the caverns and tunnels of the N'yadach. Once the war was won, their allies gave them a large district for their part in the conflict, and the two races have remained friendly to this day.

Skorn are a little over a metre high, hunched and stooped from years of mining and tunnelling. They have large, bald heads with high ridged foreheads. Their eyes are deep-set and piercing, enabling them to see well in near darkness. Their faces look distinctly like those of Hobgoblins and Orcs, though it is not thought that they are related. From the sides of their mouths poke small upturned fangs, which they use to chew up the rats and other scuttlers they live on. Their bodies are muscular and completely hairless. Skorn typically dress in short loincloths and leather-thonged sandals, with a thin stiletto-like dagger thrust through their belts. They will often be covered in dust and sweat, and carrying picks and lanterns. They are by nature relentless builders, and very territorial too. They do not take kindly to trespassers in their tunnels, and will escort them brusquely but calmly away from the area.

It is thought that Skorn are ruled over by a powerful warrior, a descendant of the heroes of their rebellion, who lives in a vast cavern encrusted with precious metals and gems and illuminated by many torches.

SKUNKBEAR

SKILL: 7   2 Attacks
STAMINA: 6
HABITAT: Forests, Hills, Caves
NUMBER ENCOUNTERED: 1–2
TYPE: Animal
REACTION: Unfriendly
INTELLIGENCE: Low

The size and fearlessness of SKUNKBEARS make them exceedingly dangerous. They are almost three metres tall when they rear up on their hind legs to attack, and are covered in shaggy black and white fur with long bushy tails. They typically make their homes in caves or hollow trees, but during the daylight hours they will roam over a wide area in search of food. They are found almost exclusively in the wild mountainous areas of Kakhabad.

Skunkbears eat most living things, typically deer and boar. Their huge claw-tipped paws are normally sufficient to cope with most creatures. If they feel threatened, however, they will use another method of attack. Turning its back on its opponent, a Skunkbear will lift its tail and squirt a nauseating secretion from a special gland. This smells so foul that its opponent will be forced to fight with 2 points temporarily removed from his SKILL as he gags on the stench. This smell also permeates the glossy pelt of the Skunkbear, unfortunately making it worthless.

SLEEPING GRASS

SKILL: 0 (see below)
STAMINA: 2
HABITAT: Wilderness, Hills, Plains
NUMBER ENCOUNTERED: 1 patch
TYPE: Plant
REACTION: Neutral
INTELLIGENCE: None

SLEEPING GRASS is not an actively carnivorous plant, but it can nevertheless greatly affect anyone encountering it. It is a fiery-red colour (a large patch of it gives Firetop Mountain its name), and produces many small flowers among its blades. The flowers emit a very sweet smell when disturbed, and fill the air with a cloud of pollen. Anyone who disturbs the grass will suddenly feel very relaxed and tired, and will stop to sit among the flowers and rest. He will feel his eyelids growing heavy, and then fall into a deep sleep full of vivid dreams for several hours. Predators sometimes wait near patches of Sleeping Grass, knowing that there is a chance of some easy prey. Unless they are very quick in dragging their victim off the patch, though, they will fall asleep themselves. It can be truly alarming to wake up surrounded by a pack of lions, Orcs and Snattacats, all fast asleep!

SLIME EATER

SKILL: 7   3 Attacks
STAMINA: 11
HABITAT: Towns (sewers), Dungeons
NUMBER ENCOUNTERED: 1–3
TYPE: Monster
REACTION: Hostile
INTELLIGENCE: Low

Its name says exactly what the SLIME EATER does: the disgusting thing delights in feeding on the foul gunge that collects in cesspools and sewers, especially under old cities like Kharé. They are huge, blubbery creatures, roughly humanoid in size, with a vast trough of a mouth, which is perfect for scooping up sludge. Their large eyes are ringed red from the overwhelming fumes of their homes, and they have a pair of short, tube-like horns which blow sulphurous steam from the tops of their heads. Their whole body is bloated and flabby, their arms and legs fat but also muscular.

Slime Eaters are very sociable creatures, and can often be found wallowing together in the muck that fills their tunnels. When one of them, foraging for food, discovers a particularly choice slurry of stinking sewage, it will bellow down the echoing tunnels for its fellows to join it for a feast. As well as slime, the creatures also enjoy fresh meat, though most of the time they have to settle for rats or Sewer Snakes, which are apparently very stringy. There is a rumour that speaks of a giant Slime Eater, served by a horde of lesser beasts, which dwells in a cavernous sewer deep below Kharé – though no one has dared test the truth of it!

SLIME SUCKER

SKILL: 10
STAMINA: 9
HABITAT: Marshes
NUMBER ENCOUNTERED: 1
TYPE: Monster
REACTION: Unfriendly
INTELLIGENCE: Low

In the stinking, black, slime-filled waters at the heart of a swamp, there live disgusting and dangerous beasts known as SLIME SUCKERS. They look like creatures out of a nightmare. Six octopus-like legs support a shapeless body, which merges into a head with huge, evil eyes and a cavernous, tooth-filled mouth. From the top of its head sprouts a pair of breathing-tubes that allow it to lurk beneath the surface of the mud, awaiting its next meal. Dark green, foul-smelling slime covers its body, and it gurgles disgustingly in anticipation of a meal.

Fighting such a creature often means standing knee-deep in mud, which will temporarily reduce the opponent's fighting SKILL by 2 points. The Slime Sucker itself has little trouble negotiating the treacherous swamps, shifting its weight from one tentacle-like leg to another while lashing out at its prey with two more. Once it has caught and killed its prey, it will drag it beneath the stinking waters, to nibble it slowly to the bone, gorging on the succulent meat.

GIANT SLUG

SKILL: 7   4 Attacks
STAMINA: 15
HABITAT: Marshes
NUMBER ENCOUNTERED: 1–2
TYPE: Mollusc
REACTION: Unfriendly
INTELLIGENCE: Low

Pale grey in colour, but spattered with foul-smelling green slime, GIANT SLUGS roam through the fetid swamps in search of suitable food, their huge bloated bodies dragging slowly through the mire. Growing to almost eight metres long and three metres across, they are vile, repulsive creatures, their boneless bodies rippling disgustingly as they slither along. They prefer to roam after sundown, for they dislike bright light, and spend their days half-submerged in mud in the shelter of the reeds.

Giant Slugs eat virtually anything edible, for they need large amounts of food to keep their huge bodies alive. When it comes to catching living things, however, they are rather too slow and ponderous. So they have developed poisonous saliva, which they are able to spit for quite a distance. The stuff will hit its victim and cause 5 points of damage to his STAMINA, unless he can dodge it by rolling his SKILL or less on two dice. A Giant Slug can only spit once every hour, so once it has done so it must close with its prey and fight by trying to catch him in its huge mouth and swallowing him whole.

SLYKK

SKILL: 6
STAMINA: 5
HABITAT: Marshes, Caves, Rivers
NUMBER ENCOUNTERED: 2–12
TYPE: Monster
REACTION: Hostile
INTELLIGENCE: Low

The SLYKK are a race of small and slimy frog-like amphibians which dwell in many places across Allansia and elsewhere. They need to live close to water, and can be found in marshland, rivers and damp caves – anywhere they can keep their skins moist and slimy. Slykk stand on their hind feet, and can grasp with their hands, but they still bear a marked resemblance to their frog ancestors. They communicate in patterns of stilted croaks, and have powerful legs and webbed feet for swimming. Their

tongues are prehensile, and they can use them to snatch small water creatures to eat, though they are useless against larger beings.

Slykk live in different tribes, each with its own distinguishing patterns and colours, which range from green and yellow to brown and black. The tribes are always feuding with one another, for a variety of petty reasons incomprehensible to non-Slykk. Warriors can sometimes be encountered on patrols on the edge of their territory, carrying crude spears and swords. Their inability to unite into one race has proved very costly to the Slykk, and the weakened tribes suffer badly from the ravages of many predators, including Giant Leeches and Kokomokoa. The tribes are ruled over by strong, over-proud chieftains, who often parade in their finery, decorated with jewels and gold stolen from human adventurers who have been caught up in one of their interminable civil wars.

SNAKE

	Poisonous Snake	Sewer Snake	Giant Snake
SKILL:	5	6	7
STAMINA:	2	7	11

HABITAT: Jungles, Deserts, Marshes, Wilderness,
　Dungeons, Ruins, Caves, Forests, Towns (sewers)
NUMBER ENCOUNTERED:
　Poisonous – 1–6
　Sewer/Giant – 1
TYPE: Reptile
REACTION: Hostile
INTELLIGENCE: Low

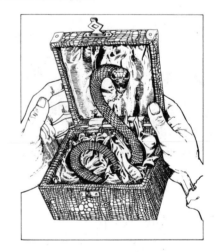

SNAKES are common creatures found in most parts of the world. While there are many harmless species, there are others that can be surprisingly dangerous. POISONOUS SNAKES come in a number of different species, ranging from fifteen centimetres to three metres long. If more than one Snake is encountered, their STAMINA scores should be added together and they will fight as a single monster. If they score a successful hit, the poison in their fangs will cause 4 points of damage instead of the usual 2.

SEWER SNAKES are powerful Snakes found only in the septic muck below ancient cities like Kharé and Blacksand. They are a disgusting grey-brown in colour, and grow up to five metres long. Their favourite method of hunting prey is to hang down from the ceiling and drop on it as it passes by. They are not venomous, but their bite can still severely injure their prey.

GIANT SNAKES are rare creatures, usually only encountered in deep water or at the heart of a large swamp. They can grow up to thirty metres in length and a metre thick. The scores above are for a creature fifteen metres long. For every extra five metres, add 1 SKILL and 3 STAMINA points (thus a Giant Snake twenty-five metres long will have SKILL 9 and STAMINA 17). If a Giant Snake scores two hits in succession, it will swallow its prey whole and he will quickly die in its powerful digestive acids.

SNAKE DEMON

SKILL: 14   2 Attacks
STAMINA: 25
HABITAT: Demonic Plane, Dungeons, Ruins
NUMBER ENCOUNTERED: 1
TYPE: Demon
REACTION: Hostile
INTELLIGENCE: High

The three SNAKE DEMONS spend much of their time slumped sullenly on their respective thrones in the great hall of their bizarre palace, arguing and bickering over every decision they have to make. The Princes, named Ishtra, Myurr and Sith, are high-ranking members of Hell's nobility, but they are somewhat lacking in the appropriate courtly airs and graces, and their discussions often end in one of them declaring war against the others. The unceasing eternity of their existence has resulted in its having long since lost all novelty – in short, they are bored. All of them are inhumanly cruel to all their servants all of the time, of course, but blasting a miserable Demonic Servant into a pile of bones lost its attraction eons ago. There is one activity, though, for which they can still muster a semblance of enthusiasm, and that is being unspeakably nasty to humans.

The Earthly machinations of Sith, in particular, sometimes shock even the most decadent Demons. It enjoys persuading all manner of races to wage pointless and bloody wars against mankind, simply for sport. Its religion, furthermore, demands sacrifices and blood-letting to appease its desire to inflict as much suffering as possible on the race of man, for it delights in seeing the puny beings squirm. It will sometimes even arrive in person to savour fully the subtle nuances of the occasion.

When appearing on the Earthly Plane, a Snake Demon will tone down its usual grisly appearance, and simply manifest itself as a greenish-black, snake-headed, four-armed, bat-winged, three-metre-tall humanoid! The aura of Evil surrounding such a monstrosity will cause all Good-hearted beings it encounters to lose 1 point of SKILL and 2 of LUCK. Like most Demon Princes, it can only be harmed by an enchanted or blessed weapon; holy water will act like acid and deliver one die of STAMINA damage to it. The four arms of a Snake Demon give it incredible dexterity in combat and allow it to deliver a second blow against an opponent each Attack Round (an adventurer successfully beating this second strike will save himself from damage, but will not inflict any himself). When appearing on this plane, a Snake Demon will be tied to its own dimension by a magical link, in the form of a gem, which holds back the elemental forces that would immediately throw the abomination back to where it came from. Smashing such a gem will instantly banish the Demon, but the explosion will deliver two dice of damage to its destroyer, unless he is well protected by magical charms and spells.

SNAPPERFISH

SKILL: 6
STAMINA: 2
HABITAT: Rivers, Lakes
NUMBER ENCOUNTERED: 1–6
TYPE: Fish
REACTION: Hostile
INTELLIGENCE: Low

The SNAPPERFISH is an infrequent hazard found in a number of locations across Allansia and beyond. Little larger than a man's hand, it is nevertheless equipped with amazingly powerful jaws and teeth like a row of fine needles. Snapperfish are savage carnivores, despite their size, and can always detect potential food when it is in the same body of water as them. Their bite is even worse than that of a Piranha, both doing physical damage and causing a great shock to their victim's nervous system: it does 3 points of STAMINA damage and 1 point of SKILL damage. Once the prey is dead, they will strip the flesh from it in a few minutes, leaving only the bare bones to drift to the bottom . . .

If he manages to hit a Snattacat, the beast will be dazed for a while, lose concentration and reappear. In the next round, it can be attacked normally, but unless the Snattacat is injured further it will blink out of sight again the round after and attack again. Once their prey has been killed, the whole pack will feast – remaining invisible to do so, a most alarming sight! – before a slight rustling in the long grass indicates that they have moved on in search of more food.

SNATTACAT

SKILL: 7   2 Attacks
STAMINA: 9
HABITAT: Forests
NUMBER ENCOUNTERED: 3–8 (1 die plus 2)
TYPE: Animal
REACTION: Unfriendly
INTELLIGENCE: Low

'As surprising as a SNATTACAT!' is an oft-used phrase across the Baklands of central Kakhabad, for the powers of a Snattacat are infamous. The beasts in question are man-eating predators, about the size of a large dog. They are covered in short black fur slashed with yellow stripes, which camouflages them in the thick undergrowth of the depths of the Forest of Snatta where they live. Their heads are like that of a tiger, but with a snub, squat snout that gives them a rather ugly appearance. Many unfortunate men and women – hunters, farmers and adventurers – can attest to the sharpness of their teeth and claws, and more . . .

Snattacats can turn themselves invisible at will, simply by closing their eyes and concentrating. They can then attack their prey without fear, hitting it automatically for 2 points of damage. Trying to hit an invisible opponent is like fighting in the dark, and will reduce an adventurer's SKILL by 2 points.

GIANT SPIDER

SKILL: 7   2 Attacks
STAMINA: 8
HABITAT: Forests, Caves, Ruins, Dungeons, Marshes, Wilderness, Deserts
NUMBER ENCOUNTERED: 1
TYPE: Insect
REACTION: Hostile
INTELLIGENCE: Low

Found in many parts of the world, from the hottest desert to the dampest swamp, GIANT SPIDERS are frightening predators. Constantly on the look-out for food, these huge black monsters grow to prodigious sizes, with bodies sometimes over a metre across. Some hunt their prey by stalking them silently before striking. Others build webs, vast sticky nets designed to entangle any creature that comes too near. Anyone caught in a Giant Spider's web must roll his current SKILL score or below on two dice *twice*, to escape its tangles. While he is struggling free, the Spider can make an automatic attack, biting deeply for 2 points of damage. Webs burn easily, though anyone caught in a blazing web will take 2 dice of STAMINA damage, unless they can escape in time.

SPIDER MAN

SKILL: 7
STAMINA: 5
HABITAT: Caves, Dungeons
NUMBER ENCOUNTERED: 1
TYPE: Insect/humanoid
REACTION: Hostile
INTELLIGENCE: Average

The strange creatures known as SPIDER MEN are the result of a particularly cruel joke played by a Demon Prince upon a coven of its acolytes. They had asked their master to change them into Death Spiders, so that they might ensnare more souls for it. On a sadistic whim, it decided to show these puny humans what a curse a spider's body could be.

Spider Men look much like a Death Spider, with a human head on top of a spider's hairy body. However, where the Death Spider's body grew to match the size of its head, the Spider Men's heads diminished to match their bodies, leaving them about ten centimetres across! Since they were loyal servants, though, their Demon Prince master endowed them with a fatal poisonous bite, before leaving them to scuttle about the world.

They are foul-tempered little things, for they begrudge everything that draws breath, and they will attack anything they encounter with a berserk fury that would be laughable in something their size were it not so serious. Should they manage to bite their opponent, their venomous fangs will inject a fatal poison that will incapacitate him in a few brief moments, and kill him quickly but painfully a little while later.

SPIRIT STALKER

SKILL: 10
STAMINA: 8
HABITAT: Ruins, Dungeons
NUMBER ENCOUNTERED: 1
TYPE: Undead
REACTION: Hostile
INTELLIGENCE: High

Animating a corpse so that it becomes a mindless Zombie requires a fair amount of magical knowledge and research, but it can be done by any sorcerer worth his staff. Creating the diabolical undead beings known as SPIRIT STALKERS, however, requires remarkable power. The last known sorcerer to possess such power was the Night Prince, Zanbar Bone – but then he was already half-undead himself.

Spirit Stalkers appear as extremely pallid, ghoulish humans, with decaying skin stretched so tightly across their bones that it has torn in many places. They will usually wear cloaks and cowls to hide their horrifying features. Unlike a Zombie, they have retained their intelligence, and will prove to be skilful opponents. The touch of a Spirit Stalker burns living flesh, for 2 points of damage to a person's STAMINA. Their deathly origins mean that they cannot be harmed by normal weapons, which will puncture and cut them but will not harm them physically. Only a weapon made from solid silver can harm a Spirit Stalker, burning its dead flesh just as its touch burns living flesh. When they finally die, their robes fall to the floor, as their bodies dissolve in a hiss of thin smoke to be blown away on the wind.

SPIT TOAD

SKILL: 5
STAMINA: 6
HABITAT: Marshes, Rivers
NUMBER ENCOUNTERED: 1
TYPE: Amphibian
REACTION: Unfriendly
INTELLIGENCE: Low

Even in the most placid and idyllic pools dangerous creatures may lurk just below the surface. The SPIT TOAD is one such peril, a man-sized amphibian that attacks by shooting a jet of acid at any creature stopping to drink at its pool. Unless the target rolls under his SKILL score (on two dice), he will be blinded by the liquid, leaving him vulnerable to the Spit Toad as it leaps out of the water and attacks with a mouth full of teeth. If its opponent has been blinded, it will automatically bite him in its first strike, causing 2 points of STAMINA damage; otherwise, the fight will proceed as normal. Should the Spit Toad kill its opponent, it will swallow him whole, before leaping back into its pool. Spit Toads are solitary creatures, and only meet up on one night a year, to mate and spawn in the moonlight before returning to the safety of their lonely pools, to wait for their next meal.

SPRITE

SKILL: 5
STAMINA: 6
HABITAT: Forests, Hills, Caves
NUMBER ENCOUNTERED: 1
TYPE: Humanoid
REACTION: Neutral
INTELLIGENCE: High

SPRITES are tiny woodland creatures thought to be related to Elvins and Pixies (they are sometimes mistakenly called Wood Pixies). They grow to about forty centimetres, and usually dress in clothes of green or brown. Their most noticeable feature is the pair of delicate, gossamer-thin wings which stretch out from their shoulders for almost half a metre. Sprites can fly well, flitting in and out of the trees of their forest home. They are peaceful creatures, and are rather shy of larger beings; they will normally try to hide when approached by a human. The only large beings they trust at all are Elves, who they know will not harm them.

If threatened, or if they are feeling especially brave and mischievous, Sprites can always resort to their magical powers. They know a number of spells, including Drowsiness, which will send its target to

sleep for a short while, and a whole host of illusions, including the creation of false treasure, and the sudden appearance of contagious boils on someone's face. Their magic is not really harmful to anyone, but can give the Sprite time to flee the area or fetch stronger help.

STING WORM

SKILL: 8
STAMINA: 7
HABITAT: Caves, Forests, Hills, Wilderness
NUMBER ENCOUNTERED: 1
TYPE: Monster
REACTION: Unfriendly
INTELLIGENCE: Low

Related, it is thought, to the Giant Sandworms of the Desert of Skulls, STING WORMS are vast predatory beasts found in isolated places across the northern lands. Their huge, segmented bodies grow up to seven metres long. Their tails are tipped with the sharp poisonous stings that give them their name. In a fight the Sting Worm will slash and stab with this; should it hit, the poisoned tip will cause 3 points of damage, instead of the usual 2.

Sting Worms trap their prey by digging large pits in the ground, with sloping sides covered in slimy secretions. Passing creatures who venture too close to the edge may lose their footing and slip down into the creature's lair, where the thing will attack hungrily! There may be many remnants of the beast's past victims at the bottom of its pit. Bones will predominate, but there may also be a few items of equipment, and maybe even some treasure.

STRANGLEBUSH

SKILL: 5   3 Attacks
STAMINA: 7
HABITAT: Forests
NUMBER ENCOUNTERED: 1–2
TYPE: Plant
REACTION: Neutral
INTELLIGENCE: Low

At the heart of the Forest of Snatta in northern Kakhabad, the STRANGLEBUSHES grow, feeding off the creatures they catch in their long, tentacle-like branches. Similar in many ways to Tangle-weed, they can control their branches, using them to entwine around limbs and drag their prey into the heart of the bush where their bodies will be absorbed. The strange plant will attack as normal, but its attempts will not appear to be doing any damage. Instead, it will just tighten its grip a little more. If its opponent has not escaped the clutches of the Stranglebush after five Attack Rounds, he will be completely immobilized and can only wait to be choked to death by the plant before his juices are squeezed out of him.

STRANGLE WEED

SKILL: 8
STAMINA: 13
HABITAT: Forests, Ruins, Jungles
NUMBER ENCOUNTERED: 1–3
TYPE: Plant
REACTION: Neutral
INTELLIGENCE: Low

STRANGLE WEED occurs in many overgrown areas, but it is most commonly found hidden among the dense thickets at the heart of Darkwood Forest. Although it looks much like the trees that surround it, it is in fact a large, vine-like creeper, and a most voracious one at that.

The main body of the plant grows up to four metres high, and can easily be mistaken for a real tree-trunk, with its rough, bark-like surface. From around the top of this thick stem as many as fifty thin tendrils droop to the ground. The Strangle Weed uses them as a fisherman would, to trap the small creatures it usually lives off.

Each tendril is about six metres long, and ends in a cluster of bright, pungent-smelling flowers. When an unsuspecting creature stops to nibble, or disturbs the tendrils in any way, the rest of the creepers lash around it. Squeezing with prodigious strength, they choke the prey to death, and then raise it to the top of the stem and squash its juices out into a shallow hollow, where they are slowly digested over the next few hours.

Strangle Weed isn't averse to snatching at anything that disturbs its creepers, and that includes humans! If an unwary adventurer should activate the tendrils, they will immediately whip around him.

While he may make the normal attack, the Strangle Weed will also automatically strangle 1 point of his STAMINA every round. If the adventurer dies, it will raise the corpse up, and slowly crush his flesh and extract his juices, leaving the skeleton hanging high above the ground. It can be very disconcerting to take a stroll through the forest and stumble on such horrific aerial graveyards!

SUMA

SKILL: 0 (see below)
STAMINA: 0 (see below)
HABITAT: Magical Planes, anywhere help is needed
NUMBER ENCOUNTERED: 1
TYPE: Magical creature
REACTION: Neutral
INTELLIGENCE: High

The SUMA are a race of generally friendly and helpful spirits, related to the more mischievous Genies. Like the latter, they live on the various Magical Planes, basking in the warm ether streams that flow in such areas. Occasionally, however, they are sent to the Earthly Plane to watch over and care for adventurers favoured by the Gods, their patrons, and help them in their fight against Evil.

Much of the aid a Suma will give to its ward is done in secret, so the adventurer is unaware of its presence. They can turn invisible at will, and will help the adventurer by making swords break, monsters slip over, arrows miss and so on. All this will simply make the adventurer think he is particularly lucky: part of a Suma's task is to make sure its aid is not noticed. Sometimes, however, an adventurer will get himself into such dire straits that the Suma is forced to materialize to help him out. A typical manifestation is in the form of a glowing, golden human, sometimes found, Genie-like, inside an object such as a lantern.

In these extremely rare encounters, Suma will usually offer verbal advice. They can tell the adventurer how to escape his present situation, though they cannot help him physically. They will never dole out the traditional 'three wishes'; such an abuse of power is left to the more Chaotic Genies, as it can radically alter Fate, which is something a servant of Good will not attempt. The advice and aid of a Suma can sometimes be rather obscure for this reason, and may infuriate an adventurer if he

moist to be burnt successfully), but while one plant is shrinking from the flames others may be gently approaching behind their prey, ready for their next meal of blood!

doesn't understand it. Attempting to attack Suma is pointless, however, for they have no physical form: they will simply blink out of existence and reappear somewhere else. They are well versed in the eccentricities of adventurers, and will be patient with them. They are well aware that the Gods of Good cannot act directly against the minions of Evil on Earth, and have to rely on the help of heroic adventurers in doing their work for them, with just a little guidance delivered by the Suma.

TANGLEWEED

SKILL: 7
STAMINA: 6 per patch
HABITAT: Plains, Forests
NUMBER ENCOUNTERED: 1–6 patches
TYPE: Plant
REACTION: Neutral
INTELLIGENCE: Low

TANGLEWEED, also known as Bloodgrass or Devil's Tongue, is a strange type of blood-sucking grass found in isolated places, often intermingled with more normal plants. It grows to almost a metre in height and is difficult to distinguish from the other grasses it grows alongside. Unlike its fellow species, however, it can control the movements of the long, blade-like leaves which it uses to catch its food. The weird plants live by entangling small animals in their leaves and sucking their blood through hundreds of tiny needle-like hairs. They are not averse to attacking larger creatures either, though a particular clump can only do a maximum of 3 points of damage before it is full up.

The leaves will usually surround their prey before the latter is aware that anything is wrong, and so the damage is automatic. If other clumps are near enough, however, they will join in the feast and may be fought as normal; if the Tangleweed wins, it will latch on and drink its fill, for 3 points of damage. Once it has drunk as much as it can, the plant will loosen its hold and sink limply to the ground, its leaves a dull red colour. Fire brandished threateningly at a plant will keep it away (it is too

TARATOR

SKILL: 8
STAMINA: 13
HABITAT: Caves, Dungeons, Hills
NUMBER ENCOUNTERED: 1
TYPE: Monster
REACTION: Hostile
INTELLIGENCE: Average–Low

TARATORS are huge, ugly beasts usually found wandering around caverns underground. They stand almost two and a half metres tall, and their fat, leathery bodies are humanoid in shape and covered in folds of grey-green skin. Their huge heads look like an unfortunate cross between a toad and a gibbon, and they have enormous mouths to serve their main occupation, which is eating.

Tarators are solitary creatures, mostly because of their foul temperaments. They stamp around their domains, snarling to themselves and cursing all existence. They will attack almost anything they take a dislike to, from Dragons to daisies, and they can be very dangerous adversaries. In a fight, their enormous clawed fists allow them to do 3 points of damage after a successful hit. However, a winning hit against them in return will do 1 point less damage than usual, because of their thick, blubbery skin. Tarators rarely stay in one place very long, for obvious reasons, and they never keep treasure, except to eat out of spite.

TENTACLED THING

SKILL: 8   3 Attacks
STAMINA: 10
HABITAT: Marshes, Rivers, Caves
NUMBER ENCOUNTERED: 1
TYPE: Monster
REACTION: Hostile
INTELLIGENCE: Low

In desolate areas, far away from the settlements of men, evil lurks writhing and gibbering in blind hatred of light and life. Unwary explorers sometimes stumble into its domain, heedless of its presence until strong, slimy tentacles lash out of the murky water and wrap around their legs. The TENTACLED THING is powerful and cunning, and will soon drag them floundering into its pool. Even the hardiest warriors find it difficult to fight for their lives when entangled in thick, crushing tentacles under several metres of filthy water. Unless the victim can kill the monstrous creature in less Attack Rounds than his current SKILL score, he will drown and be devoured. Should he manage to kill the bloated monster, he will be able to extricate himself from its lifeless coils and rise to the surface coughing and choking, but otherwise alive and safe . . . for the time being.

TOA-SUO

SKILL: 6
STAMINA: 10
HABITAT: Mountains, Ice
NUMBER ENCOUNTERED: 3–18
TYPE: Humanoid
REACTION: Unfriendly
INTELLIGENCE: Low

The mysterious race of evil, shaggy humanoids known as the TOA-SUO inhabit caves and sheltered valleys in the icy wastes north of Icefinger Mountains. They are thought to be descended from Hobgoblin stock, but have long since adapted to life in sub-zero temperatures. Standing a little under two metres tall, and almost as broad, they are covered in sleek waves of white or light grey hair, save only for their faces and the palms of their hands, which are hairless, with a leathery covering of pinky skin.

Known to some as 'Snow Devils', Toa-Suo are carnivorous, and hunt incessantly across the icy reaches of the north. They fight with their claws, but have sometimes been seen throwing rocks and small boulders when ambushing prey from above. Strong and totally fearless, they have even been known to take on Frost Giants, though many of their number might die in such an attack. After a successful skirmish, the Toa-Suo gather up the corpses of all the dead, including their own, and drag them home to be eaten. In such desolate climes, creatures can't afford to let scruples about cannibalism stop them from eating what may be their only meal for a week. A Toa-Suo's whole existence revolves around finding the next meal, and packs of them roam far and wide in search of likely food. These creatures have a keen sense of direction and smell, and are often found in the company of Snow Wolves, which they use in tracking prey.

The race is divided into a large number of small tribes, which are further split into small family groups, or 'hearths'. For the most part, individual groups have little or nothing to do with one another. They don't appear to inhabit set hunting-areas; rather, each group roams where it pleases, taking whatever it comes across. At every winter solstice, however, all the hearths gather at a peculiar crag known in southern tales as Comrak's Eye, to receive blessing from the tribal shaman. The Eye is a finger of rock, perhaps forty metres high, which is pierced at its summit by a large, eye-shaped hole three metres across. When the sun is at its highest point on that day, it shines through the Eye, and strikes a low stone altar, around which the tribes all gather. The shaman sacrifices a mountain goat or snow deer, and casts many spells for good hunting and abundant prey for the coming year.

Toa-Suo speak in a guttural language that still retains some elements of the Hobgoblin tongue (about one in twenty Hobgoblins will understand what is being said). They keep little treasure, though tribal elders may be found wearing particularly decorative necklets or amulets around their broad necks. The shaman owns a sacrificial dagger made of a sliver of pure emerald, worth about 2,000 Gold Pieces; to attain such a magnificent weapon, however, a thief would first have to kill every member of every tribe!

The characteristics are for both male and female Toa-Suo. One in every four creatures, however, will be an immature one, with SKILL 3, STAMINA 6.

GIANT TOAD

SKILL: 5
STAMINA: 7
HABITAT: Marshes, Lakes, Rivers, Jungles
NUMBER ENCOUNTERED: 1–3
TYPE: Amphibian
REACTION: Unfriendly
INTELLIGENCE: Low

GIANT TOADS may be found in many places, from the depths of the moist southern jungles to a chill pool far beneath the ground. Unlike Spit Toads, they do not need constant contact with water, but their surroundings must be fairly moist or their skin will dry and crack. They are repulsive, warty beasts, about one and a half metres high when crouched on all fours, typically coloured with mottled patches of yellow, green and brown. Their powerful hind legs allow them to hop up to ten metres at a single bound, which can often surprise an opponent. For even greater reach, the things have an extendable tongue, up to four metres long, with which they will attack. Because of the size and strength of much of its prey, however, a Giant Toad will first disable or kill, before attempting to swallow a victim. At the end of its sticky tongue there is a poison gland which means that the Toad's blows will do 4 points of damage to a person's STAMINA after a successful hit has been rolled. Once its prey is dead, the Toad will reel it in on its tongue and swallow it whole before moving on in search of more food.

TREE MAN

SKILL: 8   2 Attacks
STAMINA: 8 (see below)
HABITAT: Forests
NUMBER ENCOUNTERED: 1
TYPE: Plant/humanoid
REACTION: Unfriendly
INTELLIGENCE: Average–Low

Forests don't just 'grow': they have to be tended and cared for if they are to survive to become strong and tall with trees. The Elves, forest-dwellers themselves, have long known this, but men have only recently encountered the gardeners of the forests – the TREE MEN.

At first sight, they are all but indistinguishable from the trees that surround them. They have tall trunks, with two large branches that they use as arms, surrounded by smaller ones. Hidden in their thick, cracked bark are a mouth and a pair of small, incredibly ancient eyes. The Tree Men move slowly among their trees on large splayed roots. They are very protective of their trees, and may attack anyone harming them, or even just trespassing in the forest. In an attack they will flay about with their two main branches. Each branch can attack separately and has 8 STAMINA points. The Tree Man itself will prove far too strong to kill, but disabling both of its arms will cause it to retreat, severely injured. Just like trees, the strange humanoids are very vulnerable to fire, and they will concentrate all their efforts on putting it out, allowing their opponents to escape their clutches.

TROGLODYTE

SKILL: 5
STAMINA: 4
HABITAT: Dungeons; Caves
NUMBER ENCOUNTERED: 2–12
TYPE: Humanoid
REACTION: Unfriendly
INTELLIGENCE: Average

TROGLODYTES are a race of small, misshapen humanoids that dwell far beneath the surface in caverns and chambers hewn from the solid rock itself. They stand about a metre high, with large ears and noses which help them move about in the darkness of their subterranean domain. Despite the darkness, they have become very skilled with their small bows – hitting on a roll of 1–5 on one die, for 1 point of damage. The little humanoids also use axes, daggers and tools made from sharpened flint.

The creatures worship a vast and complex pantheon of Deities and Demons, and they have erected huge golden statues in many places underground. It is not unusual for a larger being, wandering the lightless depths, to stumble upon a huge candle-lit cave, in which hundreds of tiny forms clad only in loincloths dance excitedly around a glowing pile of gold, chanting and wailing to their inhuman Gods. Troglodytes fear surface-dwelling creatures like men, and will not hesitate to attack them. When their prey has been overpowered, though, they may decide to have some sport with him, by putting him through the Run of the Arrow. One of the Troglodytes will fire an arrow into the distance, and a captive will be allowed to walk out to the spot where it has landed. Once there, they will start to shoot at him as he tries to escape. Despite the dark, he will rarely escape the Troglodytes' arrows.

TROLL

TROLLS are large, ugly humanoids related to Ogres, Orcs, Goblins and a variety of lesser crossbreeds. They may be found in many lands, but always doing what they most enjoy – being thoroughly evil! From the civilized Troll mercenaries of Port Blacksand to the savage Trolls of the Moonstone Hills and beyond, these creatures delight in torture, death and worse. There are a number of different types of Troll, found in different areas of the world.

CAVE TROLL

SKILL: 8   2 Attacks
STAMINA: 9
HABITAT: Caves, Dungeons, Hills
NUMBER ENCOUNTERED: 1–2
TYPE: Humanoid
REACTION: Hostile
INTELLIGENCE: Low

Violent, stupid, and thus very dangerous, CAVE TROLLS are the most primitive of all Troll races. They tend to be leaner than other Trolls, their bodies lithe and muscular with long arms that end in sharpened claws. They are uglier, if that is possible, than Common Trolls, and their teeth are far larger, sticking out more like tusks from their drooling mouths. They are solitary, unsociable creatures, usually found hiding from daylight in a dark cave or passage deep underground. They are exclusively carnivorous and delight in the tender flesh of humans, but more often have to settle for stringy rat meat. Their favourite weapons are clubs and long knives, though their talons are just as effective. They hoard shiny items, attracted by their glitter, and their lairs may be crammed with all manner of glinting things, some valuable.

COMMON TROLL

SKILL: 9   2 Attacks
STAMINA: 9
HABITAT: Towns, Plains, Forests
NUMBER ENCOUNTERED: 1–3
TYPE: Humanoid
REACTION: Neutral–Hostile
INTELLIGENCE: Average–High

Once living in the wilderness like Orcs, COMMON TROLLS are mostly found in the armies of Evil, where they can practise their favourite hobbies against puny humans. There are still a few primitive tribes of Common Trolls living in rough villages in the wildlands, but even they are considerably more civilized (as Trolls go) than the average Hill or Cave Troll. If a more primitive Common Troll is encountered, its SKILL should be reduced by 2, for it will not have had the benefit of military training. Whatever their circumstances, Common Trolls are usually large and fat, taller than a human by about a head, with ugly faces and muscular limbs. They are gruff and surly creatures, but they enjoy jokes in which other beings get severely injured. Their favourite weapons are large battle-axes and warhammers.

HILL TROLL

SKILL: 9   2 Attacks
STAMINA: 10
HABITAT: Hills, Wilderness, Caves
NUMBER ENCOUNTERED: 1–6
TYPE: Humanoid
REACTION: Hostile
INTELLIGENCE: Average

The interminable wars between the Dwarfs and the HILL TROLLS have continued since before history was recorded, for the two races loathe each other. Hill Trolls are warlike beings, who provide endless hazards to travellers and settlers in the higher regions. They are the largest of all Trolls, usually dressed in furs and leathers, their long hair braided with bones and jewellery. Their favourite weapons are spears and battle-axes, and they also use shields and odd scraps of armour to protect themselves. They dwell in tribal villages high in the hills, from where they can sweep down into the valleys to attack the settlements of Dwarfs and humans alike.

SEA TROLL

SKILL: 8   2 Attacks
STAMINA: 9
HABITAT: Sea, Rivers, Lakes
NUMBER ENCOUNTERED: 1
TYPE: Humanoid
REACTION: Hostile
INTELLIGENCE: Low

SEA TROLLS dwell in large bodies of water, from deep oceans to inland lakes. They have scaly green skins, webbed hands and feet, and gills in their necks, but otherwise look much like Cave Trolls. They live on fish, but occasionally manage to overturn a boat or pluck a tasty human from a river-bank. They can only survive in air for a few minutes, but that is usually enough for them to grab someone with their claws, bite deeply into his neck, and leap back into the water with him. They are hated by Merfolk, who will try to kill the things if they stray too near to their territory. Sea Trolls make their lairs in underwater caves, often hiding them with weed for protection. Inside there may be many relics of their past victims, both bones and treasure.

VAMPIRE

SKILL: 10   3 Attacks
STAMINA: 15
HABITAT: Ruins, Dungeons, Towns
NUMBER ENCOUNTERED: 1
TYPE: Undead
REACTION: Hostile
INTELLIGENCE: High

Known to some as the Princes of Darkness, VAM-PIRES are the most feared of all undead beings.

Their evil powers and near-immortality make them very difficult to kill, and many heroic adventurers have come to grief while trying to do just that. A Vampire will usually be encountered in or near its crypt, to which it must return to hide from the sun's fatal light every dawn. When it wishes to feed, a Vampire may turn itself into a bat and fly out into the night to seek a victim.

It feeds on the warm blood of humans, which it will try to suck straight from their jugulars by biting their necks with its elongated teeth. To help it get close enough to do this, a Vampire has a powerful hypnotic gaze. Anyone caught by the red-eyed stare of a Vampire must successfully *Test for Luck*, or fall under its power, lose his own will and stand limply while the thing sucks out his blood. If a victim is bitten three times on consecutive nights, he will die and return as a Vampire himself, ready to seek out and feed off his fellow adventurers.

There are a number of ways that a Vampire can be killed. Exposing it to direct sunlight will kill the thing instantly, causing it to shrivel to dust in its cloak. A Vampire will rarely be caught in such a manner, however, since it flees to the sanctuary of its coffin at the first sign of dawn. A crucifix or clove of garlic brandished at the creature will keep it away for a few minutes only.

Attacking a Vampire with a normal weapon is not wise. A Vampire can be hit, and blows will appear to injure it. They won't in fact do any damage to the thing, however, and once the weapon is pulled out, the wounds will close again. A silver weapon can harm them. When a Vampire is killed in this way, its body will crumble to dust, but from it a bat will emerge and fly away. The bat is the Vampire's spirit, which will return to its normal form after a couple of days, and come back to extract its revenge.

The best way of killing a Vampire once and for all is to drive a stake through its heart while it sleeps during the day. To do this, of course, its coffin must be found, typically hidden in an ancient crypt beneath a graveyard. Once the stake has been driven into its heart, the Vampire will awake and then die painfully. The terrible being will remain dead until the stake is removed again, when it will return to life, unless it is beheaded and everything is burned.

GIANT VENUS FLY-TRAP

SKILL: 0 (see below)
STAMINA:
    Each jaw – 5
    Body – 10
HABITAT: Jungles
NUMBER ENCOUNTERED: 1
TYPE: Plant
REACTION: Neutral
INTELLIGENCE: None

Deep in the heart of the most forgotten parts of the eastern jungles, everything appears to have mutated. In their lush surroundings, exotic plants have grown huge, evolving gradually into specimens many times their normal size. The GIANT VENUS FLY-TRAP is very much like a standard plant, but much, much larger. They often lie close to clumps of fragrant flowers or well-used pools, where they can count on a regular supply of fresh meat.

The plant consists of a thick trunk-like body about seven metres tall, from which two to seven (1 die plus 1) tendrils sprout and lie scattered around its base. At the end of each tendril, lying hidden among the undergrowth, is an immense jaw-like leaf. Any creature, man-sized or less, coming close to one of these must successfully *Test for Luck*, or be caught as the jaws snap shut; this will do 3 points of STAMINA damage. Once inside the jaws, which will have locked so tightly they cannot be prised open, a creature's only hope of escape is to attack the fleshy insides with claws or a short dagger. Unless the victim kills the particular jaw, he will quickly die from the plant's powerful digestive acids.

Any attack on the outside of a jaw can be delivered automatically, but will deliver the damage equally to the jaw and its captive (hence, for a captive to be freed, he must lose 5 STAMINA points). Should the main body of the plant be killed, however, the jaws will go limp and release any captives they contain. Striking at the body may be difficult, if there are still jaws open and ready to attack. The remains of past victims may be found scattered among the tangled creepers that surround the plant, and there may well be metal treasures that will have been dropped from the jaws, as they are indigestible.

GIANT WASP

SKILL: 6
STAMINA: 6
HABITAT: Plains, Hills, Forests
NUMBER ENCOUNTERED: 1–3
TYPE: Insect
REACTION: Unfriendly
INTELLIGENCE: Low

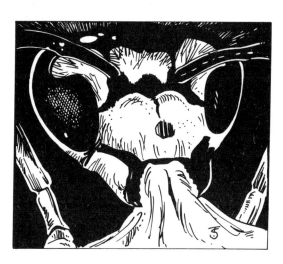

GIANT WASPS are rare but deadly insects, found in deserted sites, well away from civilization. They will attack almost anything they encounter, to feed both themselves and the larvae in their gigantic nests. They are almost two metres long from antennae to sting, with wings three metres across; they can fly at great speed, and often use a fast dive to attack. When assailing large prey, they will try to grasp it with their legs and then sting it. If an attack succeeds, they will do damage as normal, but also leave the barbed, arrow-like sting impaled in their victim. The sting's coating of poison will cause loss of a further 2 points of STAMINA and 1 point of SKILL. The insects are very afraid of fire, however, which can damage the thin membranes of their wings, and a Giant Wasp can often be driven away by nothing more than a blazing torch.

WERE-CREATURE

When the full moon hangs high in the midnight sky, some wretched humans are forced to turn into savage beasts and roam the countryside in an orgy of feasting and slaying. They are afflicted with a strange disease called Lycanthropy.

A person can catch it from being bitten by a WERE-CREATURE such as a Werewolf, for it is very contagious. Once infected with the disease, a person will become feverish after an hour, and unable to perform any actions. During this time the disease can be fought by eating a sprig of Belladonna. The poison in the plant will cause him 2 points of STAMINA damage, but he will be cured of the disease.

If this is not done, the disease will go into its second stage in another hour or so. The fever will become more severe, causing its sufferer 3 points of damage to his STAMINA. Hair will begin to sprout from his upper body, head and arms. His facial features will change dramatically, until they become the same as those of the beast that bit him, be it a Werebear, Wererat, Weretiger or Werewolf.

Were-creatures live strange double lives. During the day they will look much as they always did; but once the hours of darkness come, they can change their shape, if they wish, and go hunting. During the time of the full moon they change into their bestial *alter ego* as soon as it rises in the sky.

Were-creatures are typically taller and stronger when in beast form. Their intelligence is decreased in most cases, though, as they will become blood-crazed animals. The four types listed below are the most common, though there are said to be exotic species such as Werefoxes and Weresharks in distant lands.

WEREBEAR

SKILL: 9   3 Attacks
STAMINA: 13
HABITAT: Forests, Hills, Plains, Caves
NUMBER ENCOUNTERED: 1
TYPE: Humanoid
REACTION: Unfriendly
INTELLIGENCE: Average

The largest and strongest of all Were-creatures, WEREBEARS prefer to live in the wilds with real Bears than in the company of men. A Werebear will usually be encountered with one to six ordinary Bears, which will obey his commands, whether he himself is in human or animal form. In their human forms Werebears will tend to be large, ponderous types who are slow to anger, but very dangerous when aroused.

WERERAT

SKILL: 8
STAMINA: 6
HABITAT: Towns (sewers), Ruins, Dungeons, Caves
NUMBER ENCOUNTERED: 1–2
TYPE: Humanoid
REACTION: Unfriendly–Hostile
INTELLIGENCE: High

Unrelated to Rat Men, despite many physical similarities, WERERATS will often be found in small colonies among the maze-like tunnels of a city's sewers. Unlike other Were-creatures, they are sociable beings. The darkness of their subterranean home allows them to maintain their bestial form at all times, if they wish, which also helps them to negotiate the cramped tunnels of their home. They have a keen sense of smell, and can track their prey through total darkness, even among the pungent smells of the sewers.

WERETIGER

SKILL: 9   3 Attacks
STAMINA: 11
HABITAT: Plains, Jungles, Ruins, Towns
NUMBER ENCOUNTERED: 1
TYPE: Humanoid
REACTION: Hostile
INTELLIGENCE: Average

More common in tropical parts than in the northern lands, WERETIGERS dwell alongside normal tigers in the bush. They will usually be in the company of at least one of them when encountered, no matter which form they are in. Unlike the other types, Weretigers are predominantly female, though they lose none of their ferocity for all that.

WEREWOLF

SKILL: 8   2 Attacks
STAMINA: 9
HABITAT: Forests, Plains, Towns, Ruins, Caves
NUMBER ENCOUNTERED: 1
TYPE: Humanoid
REACTION: Hostile
INTELLIGENCE: Average

This last type is the most common of all the Were-creatures, and WEREWOLVES may be encountered in most places across the northern lands. The creatures have *two* bestial forms into which they can transform. They may turn themselves into Wolf Men, walking upright on their hind legs and using their front paws as hands. Or they may take the form of true Wolves, running on all fours to hunt with a pack of the creatures. When the full moon shines, a Werewolf will always be forced to assume this second form.

WHEELIE

SKILL: 6
STAMINA: 6
HABITAT: Caves, Ruins, Dungeons
NUMBER ENCOUNTERED: 1–3
TYPE: Humanoid
REACTION: Neutral–Unfriendly
INTELLIGENCE: Average

There are many bizarre, impossible creatures scattered across the wild land of Allansia, but WHEELIES are possibly the oddest of them all!

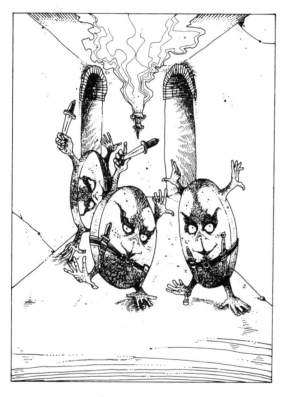

These weird creatures are disc-shaped, with large faces in the centre of one side. From around the edge of their circular bodies sprout four hands, enabling them to move by cartwheeling along! They fight with small knives, which they can launch at high speed as they tumble along on their hands. The knives will hit on a roll of 1–3 on one die, for 2 points of STAMINA damage; each Wheelie will typically be carrying two of them. But they are not so adept at hand-to-hand fighting. Wheelies can sometimes find employment in the service of a lord or wizard, for they make good guards. Many a would-be thief will think twice when faced with a few of these whirling beings, throwing speeding daggers as they spin towards him!

WIGHT

SKILL: 9
STAMINA: 6
HABITAT: Dungeons, Ruins
NUMBER ENCOUNTERED: 1
TYPE: Undead
REACTION: Hostile
INTELLIGENCE: Average

When a great and well-loved lord dies, his most devoted retainers often refuse to acknowledge his passing and continue to serve him, by guarding and keeping order in his crypt. In time they will die, but even in death their obsessive devotion may drive them to serve him. They will return as WIGHTS – bestial, inhuman things with wild hair, insane eyes and clawed fingers and toes, still dressed in their rotting livery. Wights are powerful creatures, for they are the undead servants of the dead, and can be harmed only by weapons made of solid silver. Normal weapons can hit them, but their wielders will soon realize that they are making no impression on the foul things.

Worse still, their touch is so chilling that it sorely weakens their opponents. For every three wounds a Wight inflicts on its victim, it will suck 1 SKILL point from him. Once the Wight has killed him, it will dress the corpse in ceremonial robes and sacrifice the energy it has stolen to its dead master, praying hopefully for his return to life.

WILL-O'-THE-WISP

SKILL: 10
STAMINA: 6
HABITAT: Ruins, Marshes, Hills
NUMBER ENCOUNTERED: 1–3
TYPE: Magical creature
REACTION: Hostile
INTELLIGENCE: High

Gathering in the sky above graveyards and other desolate ruins at night, WILL-O'-THE-WISPS have long been thought to be the souls of the dead, coming together to dance under the moon. Appearing as small glowing balls of light floating about in the air, they have always been associated with other undead creatures. They are, in fact, magical creatures that feed upon the very souls that they are thought to be. Related, perhaps, to Fetch, they are little spheres of energy held together by unknown forces to create a creature of great intelligence and malevolent intent.

They derive their powers from the life-forces released by creatures when they die, and as a result spend much of their time attempting to lure creatures to their death. They will dance about in the sky above them, almost as if they were beckoning their victims to follow, before leading them deep into a swamp or over a cliff! They can be hit by normal weapons, attacking in return with a bolt of energy that will cause 3 STAMINA points of damage if it hits. When killed, a Will-o'-the-Wisp will fizz away into nothing, its energy dissipating into the air.

WOLF

	Wolf	Snow Wolf	Wolfhound
SKILL:	7	8	7
STAMINA:	6	8	6

HABITAT:
 Wolf/Wolfhound – Plains, Forests, Hills, Wilderness
 Snow Wolf – Ice, Wilderness
NUMBER ENCOUNTERED: 1–6
TYPE: Animal
REACTION: Hostile
INTELLIGENCE: Average–Low

WOLVES may be found across all of the northern lands, roaming in small packs in search of food. They are perpetually hungry, and will follow their prey for many hours, until they strike at an unguarded moment. Their prey will know they are there from the eyes glinting in the darkness, and from the howling which will scare horses and other docile animals so much that they will flee unless tethered up. Fire will keep Wolves at bay, but wood burns quicker than their patience slackens; the moment the fire begins to die they will close in for the kill.

In the extreme north, the species known as SNOW WOLVES may be encountered. They are larger than normal Wolves, and are savage killers which fear nothing. Covered all over in shaggy white fur, they are all but indistinguishable from their surroundings. Only their hunger-crazed red eyes will give them away. The Toa-Suo keep trained Snow Wolves with which they hunt Yeti and Frost Giants.

WOLFHOUNDS are cross-breeds between Wolves and Dogs. About the size of a normal Wolf, but much thinner and with shorter pelts, they can make good guard-dogs if trained from cubs. Their pure animal cunning is then reinforced by ferocious devotion; they can tear an intruder limb from limb at a single word from their master.

WOODLING

SKILL: 6
STAMINA: 5
HABITAT: Forests
NUMBER ENCOUNTERED: 2–12
TYPE: Humanoid
REACTION: Neutral–Unfriendly
INTELLIGENCE: Average–High

The WOODLINGS of the Forest of Yore and other older areas of woodland are a shy race of small humans related to Sprites. Standing about a metre tall, they are quiet, almost dour in personality, and rarely associate with other creatures, considering them destructive and troublesome. Woodlings are rarely seen by man, since they dress in browns and greens, and are very adept at hiding in bushes and trees. They are alert at all times, as nervous and skittish as deer, and their acute hearing and inbuilt sixth sense mean they are never surprised by danger. Hunters and foresters have sometimes stumbled upon their settlements – circles of small huts built around tree-trunks from woven branches and roofed with large leaves – only to be repulsed by the inhabitants, who fight to the death with daggers and poisoned throwing-darts. Upon returning in force to such settlements, the men have always found them deserted, abandoned by the Woodlings for fear of being discovered again.

Occasionally, however, Woodlings are said to have helped lone humans who have been caught in poachers' traps or lost in the depths of the forests. The secretive humanoids appeared out of the trees, helped the unfortunates by freeing them or leading them to the edge of the woodland, and then melted back into the trees without a word. Such stories are rare; in many villages they appear more as legend than truth, and are believed by few.

WRAITH APE

SKILL: 7
STAMINA: 7
HABITAT: Hills, Mountains
NUMBER ENCOUNTERED: 2–4 (1–3 plus 1)
TYPE: Animal
REACTION: Hostile
INTELLIGENCE: Low

Rarely seen during the day, WRAITH APES are a fiercely territorial species of large monkey. They hunt at night, usually in packs of three or four. Left to themselves, they will avoid humans, but if they find any sort of bipedal creature trespassing on their territory while they are patrolling at night, they will attack without warning.

Their short-haired fur is as black as coal, which serves to camouflage them at night, while they stalk their territory. A sharp-eyed observer (with a SKILL of 9+) will be able to spot them just before they approach, but only by their glowing red eyes. Wraith Apes have night vision and, when they attack at night, will add 2 to their Attack Strength against any creature without night vision.

However, such an observer must be looking for them high in the trees. Wraith Apes are so called because of their method of attack. A large fold of skin under each arm allows these creatures limited powers of flight. Throwing themselves from a high perch, they are able to glide deftly down upon their victims and land accurately in front of them. To anyone who has never come across a Wraith Ape before, this frightening spectre appears as a frenzied Wraith, silhouetted against the night sky.

Wraith Apes have another dangerous ability: they have learned to use the leaves of the Blade Tree as a weapon. Blade Trees have sharp, broad-bladed leaves which grow at the ends of strong branches. The leaves themselves are as hard as rock, so these makeshift weapons are equivalent to a sharpened stone axe, and will add 1 point to the Wraith Apes' SKILL.

WRAPPER

SKILL: 12
STAMINA: 9
HABITAT: Dungeons, Caves
NUMBER ENCOUNTERED: 1
TYPE: Monster
REACTION: Hostile
INTELLIGENCE: Average

The WRAPPER is a strange, dungeon-dwelling monster that lurks in the shadows of the underworld waiting for foolhardy adventurers and unwary creatures to stumble into its lair for dinner. It is large and black, and resembles a cross between a cloak and a thick blanket. Its body is wide and leathery; its head hangs between its shoulders, down inside the span of its wings, and it has evil red eyes, a wide, fang-filled mouth and skeletal claws.

Wrappers can fly, gliding almost silently through the darkness, guided by echoes from the walls picked up by two sensitive pits above their eyes, and balanced by their long, thin tails. They can also crawl along floors and across walls using their claws, but only very slowly. Wrappers have an incredible sense of hearing, which picks up vibrations in the ground and walls as well as audible sound. They wait motionless for their prey, often flattening themselves against the ceiling or wall, so as to be all but undetectable. The Wrapper then launches itself at its victim, enfolds it in its cloak-like wings, and bites deeply into its back.

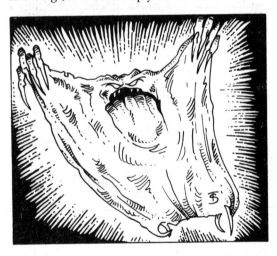

To avoid the initial attack, an adventurer must *Test for Luck* twice (once to notice the Wrapper and a second time to avoid it). If he fails, the Wrapper will gain one automatic hit (taking the usual 2 STAMINA points). Once lodged on a victim's back, the Wrapper is much harder to hit – reduce SKILL by 3 for the duration of the fight. However, hitting the beast with fire, such as a burning torch, will cause it to relinquish its hold and fall to the floor, where it can be dispatched by a single successful hit.

A Wrapper's lair will contain the skeletons of many of its previous victims, together with many fine items of treasure, looted from the adventurers who have previously served as dinner.

WYRM

SKILL: 9   3 Attacks
STAMINA: 12
HABITAT: Ice, Wilderness
NUMBER ENCOUNTERED: 1
TYPE: Monster
REACTION: Neutral–Unfriendly
INTELLIGENCE: High

WYRMS (also called Worms in some parts of the world) are solitary beasts thought to be related to Dragons. There are many similarities between the two races. Both have lizard-like heads and leathery wings. They can both live to a great age and are highly intelligent. But Wyrms are thin and snake-like, without legs and feet, and cannot actually fly.

These great white beasts dwell in icy regions where their colouring allows them to blend with their background. Their usual method of attack is to rear up on their coils, wings outstretched for balance, and blast their victim with their icy breath. This requires a successful *Test for Luck*, or the adventurer must suffer 5 points of damage. This breath can only be used once every three Attack Rounds. They can also bite their prey, but prefer to use their breath weapon as much as possible. They are cumbersome beasts and move only clumsily in combat. Their great enemies are White Dragons, with whom they often have to compete for food. Many fierce battles, unknown to man, rage in the blizzards, as two great beasts fight to the death over a scrap of food.

WYVERN

SKILL: 10   2 Attacks
STAMINA: 11
HABITAT: Hills, Forests, Caves
NUMBER ENCOUNTERED: 1
TYPE: Monster
REACTION: Hostile
INTELLIGENCE: Low

Alongside the majestic Dragons, there is another race of lesser flying creatures, known as WYVERNS. They grow at the most to ten metres long, but otherwise look very similar to Dragons, except that they have only two legs. This makes them look more like scaly birds than winged lizards.

They are typically coloured green or brown, with lighter undersides; their eyes are red, ever glinting with malevolent cunning.

Like their larger cousins, Wyverns can breathe fire from their mouths, though more as a short burst than a continuous stream of flame. Anyone finding himself under attack from a fire-breathing Wyvern must successfully *Test for Luck*, or be singed for 4 STAMINA points of damage. The great beast will then land and attack with its huge claws and fangs, and drag the corpse into its lair to be consumed.

XOROA

	Worker	Warrior
SKILL:	6	10
STAMINA:	7	11

HABITAT: *Plains, Hills, Forests, Deserts*
NUMBER ENCOUNTERED:
   Warriors – 1–6
   Workers – 2–12
TYPE: *Insect/humanoid*
REACTION: *Neutral–Unfriendly*
INTELLIGENCE: *Average–Low*

The XOROA are a strange race of mutated ant men, with the head and torso of a human and the lower body and legs of a giant ant, almost like an 'ant-centaur'. They stand about two metres tall, and are a deep red-brown colour all over. The human parts appear quite normal, but a Xoroa has no outer ears, and two flexible ant-like feelers extend forward from the top of its head. Their eyes are silver, and can see in the dark, and their sense of smell is very acute. They communicate with one another, and with the giant ants they sometimes herd, in a language made up of strange clicks and hums. The ant parts join their bodies just below the waist, allowing the Xoroa to walk on four legs, and negotiate quite rough and steep terrain with ease.

The Xoroa live in large underground colonies, visible from the surface only as a small hill of fresh earth with a large opening in the summit. The area around the colony is patrolled at all times by Xoroa Warriors, who watch over small groups of Workers, which forage for food for the whole colony. Workers are slightly smaller in height and build than the Warriors, as well as being lighter in colour and less intelligent. Warriors on guard-duty will often carry short spears and javelins, and occasionally slings. Some will also carry carved bone horns, to warn one another of approaching danger.

In their colonies there are many small, hollowed-out chambers. Some are used for storing food and equipment; others are living-quarters for the inhabitants – large, communal, straw-covered dormitories for the Workers, individual chambers for the Warriors. Most, however, are nurseries for the strange Xoroa larvae. Born from a large, bloated Queen as soft-skinned eggs, they hatch within a few hours into small, but very helpless, versions of the adult Xoroa. The queen has a dozen or so 'nursemaids' who feed and rear the young until they are able to fend for themselves. A colony can support anything up to two hundred Xoroa, of whom perhaps half will be young, and two thirds of the remaining number will be Workers.

YETI

SKILL: 10
STAMINA: 12
HABITAT: *Mountains, Ice*
NUMBER ENCOUNTERED: 1
TYPE: *Monster*
REACTION: *Unfriendly*
INTELLIGENCE: *Low*

In the desolate mountainous wastes of northern Allansia, where the snow falls thick and the wind cuts like an icy dagger, hunters huddle around their campfires and speak in hushed, fearful voices of the YETI. Their folk-tales say that long ago they were the rulers of this craggy, inhospitable land. With the coming of man and dreaded fire, the beasts retired to the higher slopes, emerging only occasionally to prey on men.

Standing more than four metres tall when rearing fully upright, these huge monsters are covered in masses of thick white fur, a pelt most prized by native hunters. Like a cross between the most savage of Apes and the most fearsome of Bears, they are equipped for hunting with a mouth brimming with sharp tusks and razor-like teeth, and paws fulls of claws each as long as a man's hand! Furthermore, their touch imparts a freezing chill that will do an additional die of STAMINA damage each time it scores a successful hit. These massive beasts are not very intelligent, but have an animal's cunning in silently tracking their prey by scent alone. They will follow an unwary man for days before choosing to strike, and when the hunter becomes the hunted there is little chance of escape! Unlike most of the mountain creatures, Yeti hibernate for only the harshest of the winter months, for they can stand all but the worst blizzards in their relentless hunt for food. When even foolhardy man stays indoors and only the inedible Toa-Suo roam abroad, they will take mountain goats and deer, but when even these become scarce they will descend the slopes and attack isolated huts. They are feared by all men, even those who take their lives in their hands to hunt these terrifying carnivores.

ZOMBIE

SKILL: 6
STAMINA: 6
HABITAT: Ruins, Dungeons
NUMBER ENCOUNTERED: 1–6
TYPE: Undead
REACTION: Hostile
INTELLIGENCE: Low

With vacant, hollow eyes staring blankly from their sickly white faces, deathly ZOMBIES shuffle around musty crypts and dungeons in the service of their necromantic masters. Unlike most undead beings, they cannot stay alive after their deaths through the strength of their life-force. Instead, their bodies are animated by a master sorcerer after a long and complicated ritual. This makes them slow and stupid, as though a part of their spirit was lost when their bodies returned to life. They cannot think for themselves, and must be commanded by their creator, if he wants them to do something besides just standing and rotting in a corner.

Zombies look very unhealthy, their pallid skin scarred and peeling, and their clothes hanging in rags, but they are strong in a fight, slashing or strangling with their clawed hands. They are slow and clumsy, though, as their every action is in response to another's command. If their master is killed, they will wander aimlessly, or continue with the last task they were commanded to do.

All Zombies can be severely injured by the careful application of holy water which has been blessed by a priest, a phial of which will cause one die of STAMINA damage, as it eats like acid into the evil things. Zombies may often be found keeping guard over hoards of treasure or important areas of a castle, for they are too slow to serve as personal servants to their evil masters.

TREASURE

There are only two reasons why an adventurer leaves the comfort and safety of his home to risk his life battling against fearsome monsters – fame and fortune. Fame comes only slowly, as a hero's deeds begin to be sung about by minstrels, or told over a mug of ale in a tavern. Fortune is easier to acquire. Many creatures hoard away all kinds of treasure in their lairs, from cheap glinting trinkets to piles of Gold Pieces, and maybe even a powerful magical artefact.

To work out what treasure a creature or a group of creatures possesses, roll one die for each creature in turn on the appropriate table according to the *Type* of the creature. Then, if necessary, roll for the amount of Gold Pieces, or for the Special Item on the lower table. This will give you the treasure, if any, that a creature has in its lair. If the creature is encountered away from its lair, it will not normally be carrying any treasure, unless it is a humanoid; in that case a roll can be made as if it was in its lair. Demons and other creatures from the Magical Planes will never have any treasure with them. Plants are assumed to be always in their lairs!

Roll	Humanoid	Monster	Undead	All others
1	none	none	none	none
2	1–3 Gold Pieces	none	none	none
3	1–6 Gold Pieces	1–3 Gold Pieces	none	none
4	2–12 Gold Pieces	1–6 Gold Pieces	1–6 Gold Pieces	none
5	Special Item	2–12 Gold Pieces	2–12 Gold Pieces	1–3 Gold Pieces
6	Special Item + 1–6 Gold Pieces	Special Item	Special Item	1–6 Gold Pieces

Special Items

Roll	Item and explanation
2	Enchanted helmet – adds 1 to SKILL when worn
3	Silver arrow – not magical, but can be useful against undead creatures
4	Potion of Invisibility – enough for one person to remain invisible for five minutes (if he attacks something, he will reappear)
5	Magical axe – this is so badly made that it will (unknown to the user) deduct 2 from his Attack Strength
6	1–6 jewels, worth 10 Gold Pieces each
7	1–3 gems, worth 25 Gold Pieces each
8	Healing potion – restores one person's STAMINA to *Initial* score
9	Magical sack – can carry five items as a single item
10	Scroll of Animal Control spell – can be used once to make up to six creatures react as if Friendly
11	Poisoned potion – causes one die of STAMINA damage to the drinker
12	Magical sword – adds 2 to user's Attack Strength

GamesMasters should feel free to substitute their own favourite items for those already on this table. Give a powerful item a high or low number, so it isn't chosen quite so often as the weaker items, and always sprinkle in a few nastier items to balance up all the nice ones!

ENCOUNTER TABLES

When adventurers are exploring an unfamiliar part of the world, there is always a possibility that they will stumble across a particular creature by chance – a random encounter. The following tables may be used when the GamesMaster decides that a wandering monster has suddenly turned up. Alternatively, they could be used when designing your own adventures: decide what the area is like, and then roll on the appropriate table to see what lives there.

Each of these tables should be used by rolling three dice on the table appropriate to the area. Adven-

turers often tend to concentrate on particular areas, such as dungeons or plains. To cater for this, there are two columns under the most common categories: simply choose which column you wish to roll on, or roll a die to decide – if the result is even, use the first table; if it is odd, use the second. A few tables have 'none' as an encounter; this means that a creature is not encountered. In desolate areas such as icy plains, creatures are few and far between; in other areas such as rivers, there are plenty of fish and other creatures, but few of them offer any threat.

DUNGEONS/RUINS

Roll	I	II
3	Mummy	Brain Slayer
4	Demon Bat	Wrapper
5	Wererat	Dark Elf
6	Skorn	Crypt Stalker
7	Skeleton War-	Iron-Eater
8	rior	Minotaur
9	Imitator	Poisonous Snake
10	Giant Rat	Skeleton Warrior
11	Orc	Giant Spider
12	Wight	Giant Centipede
13	Rock Grub	Zombie
14	Troglodyte	Doragar
15	Chestrap Beast	Ghoul
16	Manticore	Eye Stinger
17	Tarator	Night Stalker
18	Death Wraith	Phantom
	Vampire	

PLAINS

Roll	I	II
3	Cockatrice	Styracosaurus
4	Red-Eye	Weretiger
5	Mantis Man	Gark
6	Man-Orc	Giant Aardwolf
7	Felinaur	Bristle Beast
8	Hobgoblin	Common Troll
9	Wolf	Wild Boar
10	Goblin	Dwarf
11	Wild Dog	Orc
12	Centaur	Giant Wasp
13	Ogre	Rhino-Man
14	Tangleweed	Firefox
15	Werewolf	Black Elf
16	Shapechanger	Xoroa
17	Clawbeast	Werebear
18	Basilisk	Red Dragon

FOREST

Roll	I	II
3	Fog Devil	Forest Giant
4	Cat Person	Sprite
5	Werebear	Mantis Man
6	Ape Man	Dripper Plant

FOREST

Roll	I	II
7	Gnome	Elvin
8	Pixie	Skunkbear
9	Ogre	Snattacat
10	Wild Boar	Giant Spider
11	Wood Elf	Wolf
12	Werewolf	Bear
13	Poisonous Snake	Great Ape
14	Bhorket	Stranglebush
15	Tangleweed	Common Troll
16	Tree Man	Shapechanger
17	Strangle Weed	Man-Orc
18	Leprechaun	Dark Elf

CAVES

Roll	I	II
3	Banshee	Sting Worm
4	Fetch	Cyclops
5	N'yadach	Vampire Bat
6	Doragar	Rat Man
7	Grannit	Ogre
8	Skunkbear	Giant Centipede
9	Poisonous Snake	Gremlin
10	Orc	Giant Spider
11	Gargoyle	Hobgoblin
12	Great Ape	Caveman
13	Troglodyte	Jib-Jib
14	Giant Scorpion	Boulder Beast
15	Cave Troll	Rock Grub
16	Calacorm	Tarator
17	Nandibear	Cave Giant
18	Medusa	Dracon

HILLS

Roll	
3	Black Dragon
4	Shapechanger
5	Wyvern
6	Hill Giant
7	Ogre
8	Wolf

HILLS

Roll

9	Goblin
10	Dwarf
11	Hill Troll
12	Wild Hill Man
13	Werebear
14	Boulder Beast
15	Sleeping Grass
16	Bear
17	Dracon
18	Earth Demon

MOUNTAINS

Roll

3	Gold Dragon
4	Mountain Giant
5	Pegasus
6	Rock Demon
7	Giant Owl
8	Bird Man
9	Mountain Elf
10	Caveman
11	Bear
12	Dwarf
13	Giant Eagle
14	She-Satyr
15	Razorjaw
16	Yeti
17	Life-Stealer
18	Storm Giant

ICE

Roll

3	White Dragon
4	*none*
5	Frost Giant
6	*none*
7	Mammoth
8	Snow Wolf
9	*none*
10	*none*
11	Toa-Suo
12	Neanderthal
13	*none*
14	*none*
15	Wyrm
16	Yeti
17	*none*
18	Silver Dragon

DESERT

Roll

3	Giant Sandworm
4	Basilisk
5	Hamakei
6	Caarth
7	*none*
8	Fiend
9	Giant Lizard
10	Poisonous Snake
11	Sand Devil

DESERT

Roll

12	Needlefly
13	*none*
14	Giant Scorpion
15	Gretch
16	Serpent Guard
17	Decayer
18	Gold Dragon

JUNGLE

Roll

3	Tyrannosaurus
4	Weretiger
5	Giant Bat
6	Lizard Man
7	Harrun
8	Giant Venus Fly-Trap
9	Pygmy
10	Krell
11	Jaguar
12	Great Ape
13	Ape Man
14	Head-hunter
15	Bhorket
16	Black Lion
17	Giant Pitcher-Plant
18	Green Dragon

MARSH

Roll

3	Brontosaurus
4	Will-o'-the-Wisp
5	Mist Vampire
6	Spit Toad
7	Blood Eel
8	Giant Slug
9	Marsh Goblin
10	Giant Leech
11	Kokomokoa
12	Lizard Man
13	Mudclaw
14	Marsh Wraith
15	Slykk
16	Slime Sucker
17	Marsh Giant
18	Hydra

RIVERS/LAKES

Roll

3	Flying Fish
4	Fish Man
5	Giant Dragonfly
6	*none*
7	Giant Toad
8	*none*
9	Piranha
10	Crocodile
11	Snapperfish
12	Spit Toad
13	Electric Eel
14	*none*
15	Slykk

RIVERS/LAKES
Roll

16	Mudclaw
17	Giant Leech
18	Sea Troll

SEA/SEASHORE
Roll

3	Plesiosaurus
4	Sea Giant
5	Mermaid
6	*none*
7	Giant Octopus

SEA/SEASHORE
Roll

8	*none*
9	Shark
10	Giant Eel
11	Giant Crab
12	*none*
13	*none*
14	Giant Snake
15	Merman
16	Sea Troll
17	*none*
18	Water Elemental